The New Americans
Recent Immigration and American Society

Edited by
Steven J. Gold and Rubén G. Rumbaut

A Series from LFB Scholarly

Crime on the Border
Immigration and Homicide in Urban Communities

Matthew T. Lee

LFB Scholarly Publishing LLC
New York 2003

Copyright © 2003 by LFB Scholarly Publishing LLC

Library of Congress Cataloging-in-Publication Data

Lee, Matthew T.
  Crime on the border: immigration and homicide in urban communities
/Matthew T. Lee.
       p. cm. -- (The new Americans)
  Includes bibliographical references and index.
  ISBN 1-931202-70-2 (alk. paper)
  1. Crime--Sociological aspects--United States. 2. Homicide--United
States. 3. Ethnic groups--United States. 4. Alien criminals--United
States--Public opinion. 5. Emigration and immigration--Social aspects.
6. United States--Emigration and immigration. I. Title. II. New
Americans (LFB Scholarly Publishing LLC)
  HV6789.L43 2003
  364.2'5--dc22

        2003016257

ISBN 1-931202-70-2

Printed on acid-free 250-year-life paper.

Manufactured in the United States of America.

Table of Contents

v

Acknowledgements

This project would not have been possible without the active support of a large network of dedicated scholars. While the ideas found in the pages that follow were shaped in significant ways by the works I cite, my research was particularly influenced by the intellectual environment I experienced at the Sociology and Criminal Justice Department at the University of Delaware. More specifically, this book grew out of my ongoing collaboration with Ramiro Martinez, Jr., on his funded homicide research project. I am fortunate to have had the opportunity to work with such an ambitious scholar, and I am grateful for his guidance, support, and friendship over the years. I have learned from his example the importance of collecting original data and, above all, that there is no substitute for hard work in academic research.

M. David Ermann, Eric Rise, and Richard Rosenfeld, along with series editors Stephen J. Gold and Ruben G. Rumbaut, offered valuable suggestions that have improved the book. Leo Balk at LFB Scholarly was especially helpful as I prepared the manuscript for publication. Marianne Noh provided valuable editorial assistance and Shirley Wilmot helped with formatting. Finally, I wish to thank my friends and colleagues at the University of Akron's Department of Sociology, particularly Andre Christie-Mizell and Jeffrey Lucas, for their support throughout the process of revising the book for publication.

Some of the material used in this book originally appeared in the following articles:

Lee, Matthew T., and Ramiro Martinez, Jr. 2002. "Social Disorganization Revisited: Mapping the Recent Immigration and Black Homicide Relationship in Northern Miami." *Sociological Focus* 35:363-380.

Lee, Matthew T., Ramiro Martinez, Jr., and Richard B. Rosenfeld. 2001. "Does Immigration Increase Homicide?: Negative Evidence From Three Border Cities." *The Sociological Quarterly* 42:559-580.

List of Tables

List of Figures

CHAPTER 1
Introduction:
Immigration as a Criminological Concern

This book examines the relationship between ethnicity, immigration, and homicide in three "border" cities: El Paso, Miami, and San Diego.[1] This examination makes substantive, methodological, and theoretical contributions to the sociological literature on the structural covariates of violence, and has relevance for contemporary public policy debates and popular understandings of immigration and crime. Substantively, this study offers compelling empirical evidence that casts doubt on the validity of the popular stereotype of the "criminal immigrant," and the related scholarly notion that immigration (as an engine of social change) disrupts communities and facilitates crime. Methodologically, the present work demonstrates the value of count-based (Poisson) regression models for census tract-level analyses, and provides a strategy for integrating quantitative methods and qualitative mapping techniques in macrological research on violence. Theoretically, the results of this study clarify the role of ethnicity and immigration as important components of the context in which community patterns of violence are generated, thus

1

suggesting refinements of key sociological theories (e.g., social disorganization, anomie).

This study is part of an ongoing program of research that seeks to understand the complex relationship between ethnicity and homicide in cities with large Latino populations (see Martinez and Lee, 1998; Martinez and Lee, 1999; Martinez and Lee, 2000a; Lee, Martinez, and Rodriguez, 2000; Lee, Martinez, and Rosenfeld, 2001; Lee and Martinez, 2002), and utilizes data collected directly from each city's homicide investigations unit, along with data from the 1990 Census (STF3A).

Research Questions

Scholarly endeavors in the urban sociology tradition are guided by an interest in fundamental questions about social life. In this case, three core concerns motivated this research:

- Do known structural influences on homicide vary across distinct racial/ethnic groups and urban locations?

- What is the effect of recent immigration on community levels of homicide, independent of other structural factors?

- What are the implications of the answers to the above for theories of criminal violence?

Current sociological theories have difficulty accounting for variations in community patterns of violence by ethnicity and urban location, and instead hypothesize that the impact of structural conditions such as poverty should hold for all groups and locations (see Ousey, 1999:406;

Sampson and Wilson, 1995; Land, McCall, and Cohen, 1990).
In addition, the assumed positive relationship between levels of immigration and violence predicted by theory (e.g., social disorganization) has not been systematically examined with empirical data on the post-1965 wave of immigrants (see Martinez and Lee, 2000b).[2] The result is that theories of criminal violence, developed at an earlier point in time, are unable to explain the patterns of homicide currently found in the ethnically diverse urban areas of the United States. By describing, and then attempting to understand this diversity, this study updates scholarly ideas about violence so that they are better able to deal with the complicated realities of contemporary society.

The major hypothesis guiding this study is that while immigration could potentially elevate race- and ethnic-specific homicide levels in border cities where immigrants settle by increasing the level of macrosocial variables associated with homicide (e.g., economic deprivation, residential instability), it is also possible that the ties immigrants have to their jobs and families are substantial enough to overcome these effects. Therefore, consistent with most prior research on immigration and crime (see Martinez and Lee, 2000b), I expect that the percentage of recent immigrants in a neighborhood will suppress the occurrence of homicide, all other factors being equal. Since the impact of immigration on homicide can be expected to vary by ethnic group, I test this proposition using a racially/ethnically disaggregated data set (see Martinez and Lee, 1999; Hawkins, 1999a; Ousey, 1999).

Significance of the Present Study

This research is an initial effort to re-establish the study of immigration and crime as a core sociological concern.

After all, the Chicago School of sociology was founded out of an interest in the social problems (i.e. crime) that were associated with urbanization and immigration (M. Waters, 1999; Pedraza, 1996b), resulting in the first significant work of American sociological research, Thomas and Znaniecki's (1920) *The Polish Peasant in Europe and America.* Indeed, the early sociologists who wrestled with the connections between immigration and crime produced some of American sociology's most enduring conceptual and empirical work, including classics on "social disorganization" (Thomas and Znaniecki, 1920; Shaw and McKay, 1931) and "culture conflict" (Sellin, 1938; Sutherland, 1934). Despite the prominence of this line of research, sociologists have virtually ignored the relationship between the most recent wave of immigrants and crime.

Of course, debates on the immigration/ethnicity and crime linkage predate the establishment of the Chicago School, and current public discussions occur in the absence of systematically collected empirical data (cf. Brimelow, 1996; Lutton, 1996; Lamm and Imhoff, 1985). In the past, scholarly and popular ideas about the relationship between crime and the European immigrants who arrived in this country in the early 1900s centered on such contentious topics as the criminal cultural traditions of the immigrants' countries of origin, the ways acculturation adjustments encouraged criminal involvement, and the crime-facilitating characteristics of immigrant neighborhoods (see Thomas and Znaniecki 1920; for a review of this literature see Martinez and Lee, 2000b). These same ideas guide current understandings, but again, they have not been rigorously tested.

As in the past, the single point on which contemporary immigration opponents and proponents agree is that the latest wave of immigrants (largely non-European) is likely to have a more significant impact on American society than any other social issue (Suarez-Orozco, 1998; Rumbaut, Foner, and Gold, 1999; Brimelow, 1996). Yet despite both the potentially enormous impact immigration might have on crime and the high profile role of this relationship in the history of the discipline, contemporary sociological studies of the immigration/crime link have been scarce. Empirical work that does exist suggests that immigrants may be under-involved in crime, even though they experience deleterious social conditions to a degree that rivals and often surpasses the most disadvantaged native groups (Hagan and Palloni, 1998; Martinez and Lee, 2000a; Martinez, 1997).

In the absence of a sustained research agenda to assess this possibility, stereotypes will continue to guide popular understandings. Recent revelations concerning the use of racial profiling by law enforcement organizations (Harris, 2002; Verniero and Zoubek, 1999) also underscore the need for theoretically informed empirical studies of ethnicity, immigration, and crime. The lack of attention to this issue by social scientists has allowed high-profile claimsmakers (e.g., Brimelow, 1996; Lamm and Imhoff, 1985) to use anecdotal evidence (e.g., "horror stories") to construct a public identity of immigrants as a crime-prone group – a time-honored tradition in this country (see Escobar, 1999).[3] This study is among the first to empirically examine this conventional wisdom on immigration and crime, using a racially/ethnically disaggregated data set.

Preview of the Remaining Chapters

To place this study in context, Chapter 2 reviews the major theories and empirical research on homicide and focuses this general literature to provide insight into popular and scholarly writings on the relationships between ethnicity and immigration on the one hand, and homicide on the other. This discussion is needed because the variables used in this analysis were constructed based on past theory and research. This chapter provides the reader with a clear picture of the dominant popular and scholarly images of immigrants and crime -- images that the present research disputes. I pay particular attention to the role of sociological theories such as opportunity structure, cultural approaches, and social disorganization (see Martinez and Lee, 2000b; Bankston, 1998) in providing de facto support for popular stereotypes of immigrants as criminals and/or macro levels of immigration as a crime-facilitating social force.

The third chapter provides the rationale and research strategies guiding the study, and offers a detailed discussion of the data. I review the literature in order to discover guidelines for collecting and analyzing high-quality crime data in the most appropriate manner. Five strategies emerge from this review as being especially important: 1) theoretically informed data disaggregation, 2) using the most appropriate unit of analysis, 3) statistical models based on event counts, 4) spatial and temporal analyses as a compliment to the statistical models, and 5) the collection of original data. Finally, this chapter states the specific research hypotheses tested by the regression models and spatial analyses.

Chapter 4 presents a descriptive overview of each city's characteristics, as well as tract-level Poisson regression results for each city. The regression models allow an examination of the independent effects of theoretically selected variables on race-specific homicide events. Attention to each individual city's context in this chapter is important because homicide levels vary dramatically across cities, and especially across the cities examined in this study (Martinez, 2002; Martinez and Lee, 2000b). The national samples commonly used in homicide research potentially obscure important variations across local contexts.

Although the Poisson results are a useful first step, a review of group-specific homicide rates over time demonstrates the diversity of homicide involvement across groups, and casts doubt on blanket statements about the nature and extent of "Latino," or "black," or "immigrant" homicide rates (see Martinez, 2002; Martinez and Lee, 2000a; Hawkins, 1999a).[4] These rates are a function of how, for example, "Latinos" are defined (Portes and Truelove, 1987). Should Mexicans and Cubans be classified as "Latinos," or treated as distinct groups? Should Mariel and non-Mariel Cubans in Miami be treated as a unified group? Should Latinos in different cities be lumped together in future analyses?

These questions are taken up more directly in the fifth chapter, which reports the spatial and temporal findings of this study. Following Shaw and McKay (1969[1942]) and Lind (1930a, 1930b) Chapter 5 presents maps of the geographic distribution of race-specific homicide events and other key variables (e.g., the location of recent immigrants) in selected areas of each city in order to more qualitatively analyze links among ethnicity, immigration, and homicide.

Finally, the sixth chapter relates the substantive findings of this study to theories of criminal violence and suggests directions for future research. Future research on community levels of violence could profit from the lessons learned in the present study: 1) the collection of original data is essential to understand the diverse patterns criminal violence exhibited by specific racial/ethnic groups in American cities, 2) local context is an important social force shaping patterns of violence, and 3) immigration can be a stabilizing, rather than disorganizing, force in urban areas that suppresses crime. Finally, while much current research on violence is dismissed as "abstracted empiricism," I suggest that the agenda for violence research that I describe in Chapter 6 has great potential to generate theoretical insights that could advance our understanding of the basic social processes (e.g., immigration) that were once central to the establishment of American sociology as a distinct academic discipline.

CHAPTER 2

Immigration and Crime:
What Do We Know and How Do We Know It?

This chapter provides the scholarly context for the analysis that follows. Epistemologically, this study seeks to "explain" homicide in terms of community contexts, and is therefore part of the ecological tradition of urban sociology (Park, 1925a; 1925b; Shaw and McKay, 1969[1942]).

Historical Development of Theories of Crime Causation

In his classic work White Collar Crime, Edwin Sutherland (1983[1949]:7) jokingly referenced the absurd notion that "redness of hair was the cause of crime." However, just two years before Sutherland published his remarks, Hans von Hentig (1947:6) published an article titled "Redhead and Outlaw: A Study in Criminal Anthropology" in the leading criminology journal (the Journal of Criminal Law and Criminology) and advocated this very position, noting that: "It must be concluded that the number of red-headed men among the noted outlaws surpassed their rate in the normal population." Von Hentig's writings were characteristic of a criminological school of thought that explained crime in terms of traits of individuals, a perspective that helped to formulate a "scientific" causal linkage between race and crime. For example, Escobar (1999:111) notes that during the entire decade of the 1920s the Journal of Criminal Law and Criminology published only one article that offered a sociological perspective on crime causation, preferring instead to advance individualistic, often race-based theories.

In its day, this perspective (the typological school) was viewed as an improvement over earlier explanations of crime that posited either demonic possession (the spiritual school) or the absolute "freewill" to choose crime according to a pleasure/pain calculus (the hedonistic psychology school [see Lilly, Cullen, Ball, 1989; Escobar, 1999]). The typological perspective was an advance over previous criminological traditions in that it attempted to base causal explanations on systematically collected empirical data. However, the pioneering work of the Chicago school of sociology (the ecological school) beginning in the 1920s has since largely "vanquished" (Escobar, 1999:113) individualistic approaches, although neoclassical notions of rational choice and some biologically based arguments have reemerged in the last few decades (Lilly et al., 1989; Einstadter and Henry, 1995).

Pre-sociological explanations of crime fell out of favor for several reasons, not the least of which was the critically flawed methodologies used to collect and analyze the data upon which they were based (Winfree and Abadinsky, 1997; Lilly et al., 1989). These theories also could not account for variations in crime trends across communities, nor could they explain changes over time. As LaFree (1999) points out, the rapid increase in crime rates during the 1960s and 1970s cannot be linked to biological traits or psychological drives which change slowly over hundreds or thousands of years. Shaw and McKay's (1931, 1969[1942]; see also Stark, 1987) astute insight that certain neighborhoods exhibit high crime rates over time regardless of their racial composition, and despite a complete turnover in population, demonstrated the value of basing crime explanations on community context. According to this view, crime is an "environmentally structured choice" (Einstadter and Henry, 1995:133), and some environments provide more incentives and fewer disincentives for choosing crime than others. The sociological assertion that crime is "produced" by social conditions, which can change quickly and can also account for variations across communities, has therefore been the fundamental leitmotif guiding empirical studies and causal explanations for at least the last fifty years.[5]

Consistent with this line of inquiry, this book offers a "kinds of places," rather than a "kinds of people," explanation of homicide (Stark, 1987). Recent examples of this type of research emphasize the impact of structural characteristics (e.g., economic deprivation) on neighborhood levels of homicide (Parker and McCall, 1999; Land et al., 1990; Sampson, 1987). In addition to locating the current study within a particular research tradition, this discussion clarifies the epistemological stance and the nature of the questions that can be answered in terms of "explaining" versus "understanding" (Flint, 1998). While other currently popular approaches to the study of violence seek a hermeneutic understanding of the symbolic meaning violence holds for individual perpetrators (Katz, 1988; Gilligan, 1997; Lee and Martinez, 1999) my epistemological stance and methodological strategy is to explain variations in macro-level patterns of homicide in terms of their structural covariates. Having considered this issue, I now turn to a discussion of the importance of race and ethnicity in homicide research.

Race/Ethnicity and Homicide

Race and ethnicity are social constructs with constantly shifting boundaries (Hawkins, 1999a, 1999b; Portes and Truelove, 1987). Racial labels are the product of intergroup politics, not scientific evidence that there is an agreed upon set of biological or social characteristics that can be reliably used for making distinctions among groups of people (Hawkins, 1999a; Aguirre and Turner, 1998). Yet, to paraphrase Thomas (1966[1931]:301) "if people define race as real, it is real in its consequences." In other words, partly because people believe that some groups are biologically distinctive, they have treated them differently (Aguirre and Turner, 1998). Thus racial and ethnic minorities have often confronted deleterious social conditions due to prejudice and discrimination, with the effect that the experience of crime for these groups has differed greatly from that of the white majority (Shihadeh and Flynn, 1996; Massey, 1995).

On this point, a comparison of the homicide involvement of Italians and blacks in Philadelphia in the early part of this century is particularly instructive (see Lane, 1989:71-73). From 1900 until just before 1920, Italians had much higher rates of imprisonment for murder than blacks. However, as Italians were incorporated into the labor market, by the 1920s their homicide involvement declined substantially – well below that of blacks who faced continuing economic exclusion. In the span of two decades, Italians in Philadelphia moved into a position of economic stability and in so doing began to alter their collective identity away from that of a distinct immigrant group and towards being part of the "white" majority. Blacks continue to face discrimination, economic and otherwise, and still exhibit high rates of homicide in Philadelphia (Lane, 1986).

Chicago school sociologists in the 1930s and 1940s were among the first to challenge biological constructions of race, and in particular the prevailing notion that some racial groups were inferior and crime prone, preferring instead to group people according to social definitions of ethnicity. Although they were unusually progressive in this regard, their writings were characterized by a "theme of conservatism" (Einstadter and Henry, 1995:128) due to an uncritical acceptance of consensus models of law and crime, as well as their argument that immigrants and ethnic minorities engaged in crime because of their flawed cultures. So despite disagreeing with the mental testers and eugenicists of the typological school that minorities were biologically inferior, the equally deterministic writings of the "ethnicity theorists" of the ecological school reinforced the popular notion that minorities were different from whites by drawing attention to their "inferior cultures" (Musolf, 1998:57; Escobar, 1999:10). Thomas, Park, and Miller (1966[1921]:197), for example, feared "importing large numbers of aliens, representing various types, in the main below our cultural level," arguing that "they bring a greater and more violent unrest than we know here."[6]

Regardless of the ethnocentric undertones of the ethnicity theorists, their work has demonstrated the enduring value of examining group-specific crime patterns. More contemporary research has repeatedly found empirical differences in homicide involvement by race/ethnicity, and in the structural factors shaping this involvement (Parker and McCall, 1999; Ousey, 1999; Hawkins, 1999a; Martinez and Lee, 1998; Sampson and Lauritsen, 1997; Alba, Logan, and Bellair, 1994). One trend that has remained robust over time is that racial and ethnic disparities in levels of homicide are associated with enduring patterns of economic, political, and social inequality (Hawkins, 1999b; Tonry, 1995). Thus, exploring racial patterns in homicide research continues to make empirical sense, as long as researchers are mindful of the way race is constructed.[7]

Most studies of homicide, for example, have examined only "blacks" and "whites," coding Latinos and Anglos as "white" and people of both Caribbean and African origin as "black." This is largely a result of relying on the FBI's Uniform Crime Reports as the primary source of data, since the FBI does not collect more detailed information on ethnicity (Martinez and Lee, 1999). Increasingly, researchers have documented the value of moving beyond the traditional black/white dichotomy by studying the homicide patterns of Latinos (Block, 1993; Lee, Martinez, and Fernandez, 2000) and Caribbean blacks such as Jamaicans and Haitians (Martinez and Lee, 2000a; Martinez and Lee, 1998). In general, blacks tend to have the highest rates of homicide and whites the lowest, while Latinos fall in between (Hawkins, 1999a; Martinez and Lee, 1999). Yet Martinez and Lee (1999) have shown that Latino rates vary widely depending on local context, and at some time points are lower than white rates.

The causal mechanisms that might account for this variation are poorly understood, as researchers have only recently begun to question the "racial invariance assumption" that structural factors equally effect violence levels across racial and ethnic groups (Ousey, 1999). One study, for example, found that measures of economic deprivation (e.g., poverty, unemployment) have a stronger association with city level homicide rates for whites than for blacks, suggesting to its author the need to explore the role of cultural forces in black communities (Ousey, 1999). Another study discovered that the impact of the structural covariates of homicide not only varied by race, but also depended on whether the victim and offender in each incident were of a similar or different race (Parker and

McCall, 1999). However, both of these studies relied on national samples and coded only black and white race categories; a finer-grained analysis of ethnicity would likely yield an even more complicated picture. Such a study would clearly have relevance for social policies and current theories of homicide, both of which continue to rely on the racial invariance assumption.

Having considered ethnicity, the final sections of this chapter offer a more specific focus on the issue of immigration. I first discuss popular images of immigrants and crime, and then turn to scholarly work on the topic.

Popular and Pre-Sociological Images of Immigrants and Crime

> It is probably true throughout the world that most immigrant groups commit crimes at a higher rate than the general population (Lamm and Imhoff, 1985:53).

Popular opinions have assumed a strong link between immigration and crime throughout this century -- an idea legitimated by early twentieth century criminological theories emanating from the "typological" schools of thought that included Lambrosians, mental testers, and psychiatrists (Escobar, 1999:110). As Ferracuti (1968:190; see also Jaret, 1999; Short, 1997; Abbott, 1931) points out, in the first half of this century "popular opinion often expressed the view that migrants were responsible for a large fraction of the crime rate," despite considerable empirical evidence that they were not.[8] Disingenuous proclamations from law enforcement officials, along with lurid and misleading newspaper stories, often fueled public sentiment (Escobar, 1999). Statements like the following from a turn-of-the-century New York City Police

Commissioner were typical: "something like 85 out of one hundred of our criminals should be found to be of exotic origin" (Simon, 1985:70-71). This Commissioner viewed Italians as particularly dangerous "malefactors" (Simon, 1985:71) and promoted the view that the French and Belgians organized white slavery rackets.

The idea of criminal immigrants was not a product of the 20th century; a series of articles in the New York Times published in 1880 was concerned with criminal Italians, a particularly "clannish race," and the prototypical "bad Irish boy [who was] about as unwholesome a product as was ever reared in any body politic" (Simon, 1985:186). Note also that the 1892 Democratic Party platform nodded approvingly at legislation designed to keep the United States from "being used as a dumping ground for known criminals" from Europe and China (Simon, 1985:18). Such views had long been reflected in scholarly writings as well. For example, an article by William Jeffrey in an 1893 issue of the Journal of Political Economy also blamed immigrants for increasing crime rates (Simon, 1985).

This image appeared in prominent periodicals throughout the first wave of immigration. A 1915 editorial in the North American Review called for a restriction of immigration on the grounds of the "criminal and economic worthlessness" of southern European immigrants (Simon, 1985:71). Articles in other popular magazines also expressed the low public opinion in which immigrants were held. One 1923 issue of the Saturday Evening Post viewed immigrants from southeastern Europe (e.g., Italy, Greece) as the "dullest and dumbest people in Europe," while another from the same year quoted eugenicist Harry Laughlin as saying "If America doesn't keep out the queer alien mongrelized people of Southern and Easter Europe, her crop of citizens will eventually be dwarfed and mongrelized in turn" (Simon, 1985:85). The assumed criminal nature of immigrants is a common theme in these writings, with authors claiming that immigrants were filling penitentiaries and insane asylums faster than the native-born. During the 1920s, Italians, Jews, Poles, Russians, Greeks, and others were commonly portrayed as criminals.

Legislators in the 1920s were quick to use the now-discredited writings of eugenicists to craft exclusionary immigration laws in the interest of preventing supposedly inferior and criminally inclined immigrants from contaminating the native population (Sellin, 1938). In fact, the construction of a public identity of particular immigrant groups as crime-prone has been an operative goal of law enforcement organizations throughout this century. Consider two examples: the Los Angeles Police Department's promotion of the stereotype of Mexicans as criminals that facilitated anti-Mexican riots in the 1940s (Escobar, 1999), and the Federal Bureau of Narcotics' (FBN) demonization of Mexicans as uncontrollably violent when under the influence of marijuana, as part of its anti-marijuana campaign in this same time period (McWilliams, 1990). In the pre-WWII era, one LAPD police chief contradicted official statistics compiled by his own department in publicly claiming that immigrants were to blame for "most of our crime problem" (quoted in Escobar, 1999:89). Media reports also facilitated the image of dangerous immigrants, and the stereotypes guiding crime reporting are evident in this letter from the editor of a Colorado paper to FBN chief Harry Anslinger during the FBN's war on marijuana:

> I wish I could show you what a small marihuana [sic] cigarette does to one of our degenerate Spanish speaking residents. That's why our problem is so great; the greatest percentage of our population is composed of Spanish speaking persons, most of

whom are low mentally, because of social and racial conditions (quoted in McWilliams, 1990:53).

Even in the 1970s, Swigert and Farrell (1977:19) found that the stereotype of the "normal primitive" continued to guide the legal system's processing of immigrant and minority homicide defendants, as shown by this excerpt from a clinical report to the court:

> ... the designation "normal primitive" constitutes a social description of a group of people whose behavior, within their own social group, is best described as normal. The "normal primitive" comes largely from the foreign-born and black populations.... The personality characteristics of the "normal primitive" are childlike or juvenile.... Compelled to fight any challenger to his masculinity or courage, the "normal primitive" protects himself by carrying a lethal weapon.

Contemporary anti-immigrant sentiment is often promoted by organized interest groups which accuse Third World nations of exporting their excessive numbers to the United States (Simon 1993:69). And as in the past (see Sellin, 1938), current legislation – such as California's Proposition 187 and the U.S. Congress 1996 Immigration Reform bill – has not relied on scholarly research even though it has been justified on the grounds that it will stem the tide of "criminal aliens," who are a growing presence in the criminal justice system (U.S. Commission on Immigration Reform, 1994; Scalia, 1996).

Similarly, in a national best-selling book promising "common sense about America's immigration disaster," a writer at Forbes and National Review magazines states: "immigration is not the only cause of crime. It may not even be the major cause of crime. But it is a factor" (Brimelow, 1996:182, emphasis in original).[9] Hailed as a "non-fiction horror story of a nation that is willfully but blindly pursuing a course of national suicide" (Todd, cited in the front matter of Brimelow, 1996), such alarmist writings assume a strong link between immigrants and crime while providing little empirical data. In fact, Brimelow (1996:182) claims that "there has been no serious academic study of the impact on crime" of the post-1965 wave of immigration.

In another example, while governor of Colorado, Richard Lamm devoted an entire chapter of his book The Immigration Time Bomb to a discussion of the "lawlessness" of the recent wave of immigrants, at one point remarking that "there is good evidence that 40 percent of [Mariel immigrants in Miami] were criminals or had histories of criminal behavior or of mental illness" (Lamm and Imhoff, 1985:49). Of course this "good evidence" is never explicitly discussed in the book, which relies instead on a few horror stories to make its point, a long-standing tradition in the social construction of social problems.

Recent investigations of racial profiling by law enforcement organizations have shown that stereotypes of immigrants and minorities continue to guide criminal justice practices. For example, one state-sponsored study of traffic stops on the New Jersey Turnpike revealed that the "overwhelming majority" (Verniero and Zoubek, 1999:27) of vehicle searches involved blacks or Latinos and that this was a result of "de facto discrimination" (p. 7) by state troopers based on the motorist's "race, ethnicity, or national origin in conjunction with other factors" (p. 5). The New Jersey study points to the "truly national scope of the problem," citing similar revelations in other states, and blames racial profiling, in part, on "training and information-sharing programs administered by the DEA and other federal agencies" (p. 60). The Eighth Circuit Court of Appeals upheld the constitutionality of the practice in *United States v. Weaver* (1992; see Verniero and Zoubeck, 1999), arguing that "objective" crime statistics justified using race/ethnicity as a partial basis for increased scrutiny of potential crime suspects (Harris, 2002; see Verniero and Zoubek, 1999:65-75, on the tautological nature of "objective" statistics).

A recent study of the San Diego border area by Gonzales (1996) is particularly relevant to this discussion of the immigrant/crime link. He found that popular and governmental concern about the costs criminal immigrants impose on the criminal justice system (i.e., increased law enforcement, costs of incarceration) generated renewed interest in deporting criminal aliens in the early 1990s (see Escobar, 1999, for the cyclical nature of this issue). One prominent government study estimated the criminal justice system costs for undocumented immigrants in San Diego county at $105 million annually, again fueling the stereotype of the criminal immigrant. Yet this study has been heavily criticized on methodological grounds, and possibly over-estimates the annual cost by $90 million (Gonzales, 1996).

In addition, according to Gonzales (1996:168), the "vast majority of [the] acts of violence on the Mexican border can be attributed to a particular segment of the alien population," but this violence was almost exclusively directed towards other immigrants and was sharply reduced by increased law enforcement efforts in the 1980s and 1990s. Nevertheless, Gonzales (1996:163) expresses a popular opinion by claiming that "not all of the undocumented persons who cross into the United States are criminals; however, there are segments of this population which are prone to criminal activity." The empirical question of the impact of individual "criminal" immigrants, or the generic social process of immigration, on levels of crime in San Diego, or any other U.S. city, was left unanswered by this study. In order to begin to address this question, I now turn to scholarly writings on immigration and crime.

Sociological Theory and Research on Immigrants and Crime

The enormous amount of delinquency, juvenile and adult [in urban communities]... is due in part, though not entirely, to the fact that migrants are not able to accommodate themselves at once to a new and relatively strange environment (Park, 1925a:108).

It is the immigrants who have maintained in this country their simple village religions and mutual aid organizations who have been most able to withstand the shock of the new environment (Park, 1925b:121).

These quotes from a classic work of the Chicago School exemplify the contradictory views scholars have held about the immigrants and crime. And although the bulk of research on the first generation of immigrants (i.e. Europeans such as Italians and the Irish arriving in the first decades of the 20th century) found that immigrants were generally less involved in crime than natives, the stereotype of the criminal immigrant has persisted in this country (Martinez and Lee, 2000b; Jaret, 1999).[10]

With few exceptions (e.g., Butcher and Piehl 1997, 1998; Hagan and Palloni, 1999; 1998; Martinez and Lee, 2000a; Lee et al., 2001), researchers have not systematically investigated the impact on crime of the most recent wave of immigrants, drawn largely from Latin America, Asia, and the Caribbean (Kibria, 2002). The small number of available contemporary studies echo the findings of early research that found that immigrants are not particularly crime-prone relative to the native-born, yet public opinion of recent immigrants remains low and stereotypes endure (Martinez and Lee, 2000b; Mears, 2001).

While contemporary empirical studies are scarce, well-established sociological perspectives on crime continue to provide the theoretical underpinnings for the popular image of immigrants as a high-crime group. Few scholars today take seriously the once-popular view that immigrants are biologically deficient, and therefore inherently criminally disposed, but practically all of the major theories of crime would predict that recent immigrants should exhibit the highest crime rates. To illustrate this I briefly sketch the implications for the immigrant/crime link of the three leading perspectives: opportunity structure, cultural, and social disorganization (see Martinez and Lee, 2000b; Bankston, 1998). Of course explanations usually draw on several theoretical elements (e.g., Shaw and McKay's writings appear in all three sections below), and it is surely an analytical contrivance to think that "cultural" factors can be separated from their "structural" contexts, but most studies emphasize one perspective over the others.

Opportunity Structure

Opportunity structure theories stress the material and social structures that shape the values and activities of groups in American society (Bankston, 1998). Because legitimate opportunities for wealth and social status are not equally available to all groups, some will "innovate" by taking advantage of available illegitimate opportunities. This type of explanation was popularized by Merton (1938, see also Messner and Rosenfeld, 1997) and draws attention to the ways in which disadvantaged groups (which often includes immigrants) may be denied the legitimate means (e.g., jobs) to attain culturally prescribed goals (e.g., a middle class lifestyle).[11] Cloward and Ohlin (1960) added the notion that some groups, particularly those living in "high-crime" urban areas, have more illegitimate opportunities than others.

Scholars have long observed the tendency for new immigrants to settle in urban neighborhoods characterized by poverty, substandard housing, poor schools, and high crime rates (Thomas and Znaniecki, 1920; Taylor, 1931; Shaw and McKay, 1931; Hagan and Palloni, 1998). Segregated in such neighborhoods, immigrants might be expected to turn to crime as a means to overcome blocked economic opportunities, or organized crime to gain a foothold in politics (Whyte, 1943). Other writers have suggested that previously non-criminal immigrant groups may simply be "contaminated" by the abundance of criminal opportunities provided by natives that abound in the neighborhoods in which immigrants settle (Lambert 1970:284; compare Sampson and Lauritsen, 1997 on the "proximity" hypothesis).

According to this view, immigrant criminality is a function of pre-existing structural factors like poverty (Yeager, 1997), a preponderance of young, unattached males (Taft, 1936; Gurr, 1989), or the greater availability of alcohol in immigrant neighborhoods (see Alaniz, Cartmill, and Parker, 1998). In a classic study, Shaw and McKay (1969[1942]) discovered that immigrant groups exhibited high delinquency rates only so long as they resided in the most structurally disadvantaged neighborhoods. As each group moved out of these areas over a period of a few decades, their delinquency rates fell markedly, while the next group to settle in slum areas, in turn, displayed high rates.

Cultural Perspectives

In addition to this list of structural issues, scholars have viewed cultural forces as influencing criminal involvement, and immigrant crime in particular. The "culture of poverty" thesis –– where low-income people adapt to their structural conditions in ways that perpetuate their disadvantaged condition –– is one example of a cultural explanation (Lewis, 1965). Thus, engaging in crime as a means of acquiring social status draws children away from schoolwork which reduces the probability of future economic advancement. In a similar vein, Bourgois (1995:9) points out that "although street culture emerges out of a personal search for dignity and a rejection of racism and subjugation, it ultimately becomes an active agent in personal degradation."

Shaw and McKay (1969[1942]:173) added a concern with the spatial distribution of such "cultures" arguing that certain neighborhoods are characterized by "the existence of a coherent system of values supporting delinquent acts." Because immigrants (like ethnic minorities) are more likely than native whites to reside in areas where structural conditions have altered the status systems away from the middle class "ideal" and toward a culture of opposition (Bourgois, 1995; Anderson, 1990, 1999; Rose and McClain, 1990), these cultural theories suggest that immigrants should be highly involved in crime.[12]

Another prominent strain of cultural theory that is especially well-suited to the immigration/crime relationship developed out of Sellin's (1938) writings on "culture conflict." Sellin (1938:21) recognized that the criminal law reflects the values of the "dominant interest groups" in society, and that the values of other social groups, particularly immigrants, were sometimes quite different. In cases in which the cultural codes of subordinate and dominant groups conflict, legal agents label as deviant the behavior of members of the subordinate classes. Nevertheless, the criminal may be acting according to subculturally accepted norms and feel no "mental conflict" when violating the law. Thomas (1966[1927]:166) agrees:

There are always constitutional inferiors and divergent personalities in any society who do not adjust, but the mass of delinquency, crime, and emotional instability is the result of conflicting definitions.

Thus immigrants may violate the law more often than natives due to conflicts at the level of cultural codes, and associated problems of acculturation in a new environment characterized by heterogeneous conduct norms (see Y. Lee, 1998 for an example of research on acculturation and delinquency).[13]

Social Disorganization

... most of the delinquents in Chicago have been produced... by the newest large immigrant or migrant groups in the city. During the first decades of this century a large proportion of the delinquents were the children of German or Irish immigrants. Thirty years later a large proportion of the offenders were the children of the Polish and Italian immigrants who replaced the German and the Irish in the inner-city areas (Shaw and McKay, 1969[1942]:374).

The social disorganization perspective, while not denying the importance of cultural or structural forces, adds to the other perspectives a concern with the breakdown of community social institutions that results from social change. Bursik (1988:521) concisely describes disorganized areas as possessing an "inability to realize the common values of their residents or solve commonly expressed problems." In organized neighborhoods, local community institutions work together to realize community goals, protect values, and generally control the behavior of community members in ways that conform to these goals and values. Bankston (1998) notes that immigration may undermine established institutions via a process of population turnover, while it also makes agreement about common values more difficult (see also Shaw and McKay, 1969[1942]). The implication is that when social control is weakened in this manner crime will flourish.

One early influential statement of this perspective was set forth by Thomas and Znaniecki in their five volume work The Polish Peasant in Europe and America. Thomas and Znaniecki wrote about the many social changes affecting Polish peasants in this time period, including the disorganizing influences inherent in moving from simple, homogeneous, rural areas of Poland to the complex, heterogeneous, urban areas of the United States. They defined social disorganization as "a decrease of the influence of existing social rules of behavior upon individual members of the group" (Thomas and Znaniecki, 1920:2). The effectiveness of social rules (e.g., laws) derived from the individual's investment in them (e.g., attitudes favorable to laws). In the organized society, there was a congruence between group rules and individual attitudes. Disorganization implied a gap between rules and attitudes, such that an individual did not feel bound by the rules and was free to disobey them (e.g., engage in crime).

Viewed in this light, disorganization was a neutral term that suggested the possibility of social change, both positive and negative, and individual liberation from oppressive community standards, although it has generally been applied to studies of crime. One contribution to this literature is the recognition that crime is not only a function of structural (e.g., poverty) or cultural (e.g., "subculture of violence") forces, but is intimately tied to the fundamental processes of social change. Immigration, as a major agent of social change, would therefore be expected to inflate levels of crime due to its disorganizing influence on community institutions.[14]

The Counter-Claim

There are good sociological reasons, then, for anticipating a positive association between levels of immigration and crime. Immigration may be criminogenic through its association with economic disadvantage, conflicting conduct norms, weakened social control or a combination of economic, cultural, and institutional factors. There are equally good reasons, however, for questioning the standard sociological images of immigration and crime. In fact, current public discourse on the effect of immigration on urban areas is beginning to portray immigration as a positive, stabilizing force. For example, on a recent broadcast of *Talk of the Nation* on National Public Radio (2001:2,16), one panelist (Dr. William Frey, a demographer with the University of Michigan) articulated the position that cities with a high proportion of recent immigrants are experiencing a rebirth:

> immigrant cities and the high-tech cities are the ones that are going to be the shining stars of the future.... the ones that are breathing and growing... and living are the immigrant cities, the immigrant magnet cities. This is what had made cities to begin

with in this country, and I think a lot of these areas
are the ones that are really going to breed that
diversity and that vitality and that sense of
community in ways that many of the other cities
don't have.

Far from being a disorganizing and possibly criminogenic
force, this view posits immigration as an essential
ingredient contributing to the continued viability of urban
areas that had experienced population decline and
community decay in previous decades.

In this multivariate analysis presented in this book, I
evaluate the counter-claim to the proposition that
immigration increases crime.   Strong ties to the labor
market and family, I argue, offset the potential crime-
producing consequences of disadvantage, culture conflict,
and community instability, and thereby suppress the level
of crime in immigrant communities. Specifically, I test the
hypothesis that *communities with higher proportions of
recent immigrants, other things equal, will exhibit lower
levels of criminal homicide.*

Although several recent studies have called into
question the immigration-begets-crime thesis (Butcher and
Piehl, 1997; 1998; Hagan and Palloni, 1999; Martinez,
2000; Yeager, 2002), and even classic works failed to find
a consistent empirical link between immigration and crime
(T. Waters, 1999; Martinez and Lee, 2000b), scholarship
that directly investigates the contemporary
immigration/crime link is currently in short supply. It is
certainly plausible to hypothesize that non-citizen
immigrants may be deterred from crime by the potential
threat of deportation, thus helping to suppress crime in
immigrant neighborhoods. But in addition to this line of
reasoning, existing research unrelated to crime offers
substantial indirect support of our counter-claim. For

example, Portes and Stepick (1993) found that rather than disorganizing communities, immigrants stabilized and revitalized Miami's economic and cultural institutions.

The implication is that community social control may actually be strengthened by immigration, an image that is at odds with criminological theory. In fact, sociologists have long argued against the "myth" (Portes, 2000:5) that residents of impoverished urban areas are poor (or victimized by criminals) because they are "disorganized" in the sense that they lack common values or strong ties to each other.

Turning to attachments to the labor market, Zhang and Sanders (1999) found that immigrants with low-paying jobs may have a greater work incentive than similarly situated natives due to different frames of reference. In effect, the experience of being socialized in a relatively impoverished homeland results in immigrants placing a greater value on jobs than natives who were socialized in the richer host country. Immigrants therefore work longer hours than natives, even co-ethnic natives (e.g., Mexican immigrants work more hours than American-born Latinos); they also perceive more opportunities for upward mobility, which in turn may lead to high rates of upward mobility vis-à-vis similarly situated native groups (Zhang and Sanders, 1999). These perceptions are shaped by the availability of social networks and opportunity structures, with immigrants possibly having greater access to these resources than segregated native-born black populations. For example, some immigrant groups (e.g., Koreans) arrive in the United States better educated than the average American, and therefore more qualified to find jobs in the primary labor market (Alba and Nee, 1997). In some cases, immigrants have structural supports that are lacking among natives, such as "transnational networks" or the existence of "ethnic enclaves" that facilitate social and economic stability

(Portes, 1997; Logan, Alba, Dill, and Zhou, 2000). Finally, some immigrant groups have been found to be particularly entrepreneurial, such as Cubans in Miami or Koreans in southern California (Logan et al., 2000). All of this implies that immigrants may not display cultural adaptations to structural inequality (i.e., crime) to the extent of disadvantaged native groups, because of immigrants' social capital or differential experiences of relative deprivation.

Another suggestive line of research focuses on perceptions of social justice (National Consortium on Violence Research, 2000). The guiding hypothesis of this work is that persons who believe society to be fundamentally unjust will be more likely to break the law than those who believe that society is generally fair. For example, African Americans' experiences of racism and inequality may lead to a sense of social injustice, which in turn plays a mediating role in this group's disproportionate involvement in crime. Immigrants, while also subject to discrimination and deleterious social conditions, may perceive less injustice than African Americans due to different socialization experiences, or perhaps a greater sense of optimism about their prospects for advancement in American society. While immigrant-specific data on this issue are not available, one recent study of southern California did find that Latinos were more likely than either whites or African Americans to believe in a just world (Hunt, 2000).

These examples are part of a growing body of literature that supports images at odds with standard criminological notions of immigration as a process that facilitates crime. Given the potential for refining theory and informing policy – coupled with the fact that the experiences of recent immigrants (criminal or otherwise) cannot be inferred from those of previous waves (Portes 1997) – an empirical test of our counter-claim is long overdue. I therefore assess the effect of immigration on homicide across three cities that serve as major destinations for immigrants. I focus on Latino and non-Latino black homicide, since these two groups exhibit both elevated homicide involvement, high levels of economic disadvantage, and other adverse structural conditions. Immigrant Latinos also tend to settle in older Latino neighborhoods, many of which are growing into adjacent non-Latino black communities. This approach allows me to examine differences in the direction and magnitude of the immigration effect for the different ethnic groups, and ethnic differences in the covariates of homicide, such as economic disadvantage and community instability.

In addition, by estimating the effect of immigrant populations, comprised largely of Latinos, on the homicide risk of African-Americans, I can assess the *contextual* influence of immigration in urban communities. Immigration may directly influence the crime rates within the immigrant population, but it also may indirectly affect those of other groups by changing the community context in which immigrant and non-immigrant populations are situated. For example, if high levels of immigration impede communication and value consensus in a community, social disorganization theory would predict a general increase in crime and not simply increased criminal involvement of immigrants. The data used in this study, then, provide an unique opportunity to move considerably beyond the narrow focus of prior research on the crime rates of immigrant groups to assess the broader community impacts of immigration.

Conclusion

Three main points have emerged from this literature review. The first is that this study builds on a long-standing tradition in criminological inquiry often referred to as the ecological perspective. Research of this kind seeks to answer the question: "how can rates of crime be explained in terms of community conditions?" Sociological approaches currently dominate the study of homicide because of their ability to explain variations in homicide patterns over time and across communities. Within sociology, the ecological school continues to be at the forefront of theoretical developments and potentially has the most to offer policymakers.

The second point is that recent empirical work has challenged the racial invariance assumption (that structural factors influence all racial/ethnic groups equally). Given the vastly different experiences of distinct groups, a strategy of racial disaggregation is warranted. Since the focus of this study concerns the impact of immigration on homicide in border cities, the usual black/white dichotomy does not seem appropriate. Rather, this study must examine Latinos' patterns of homicide, separate from those of whites and blacks.

Third, while both popular images and sociological theories would predict a positive effect of immigration on levels of homicide, empirical research has often found the opposite pattern.[15] Unfortunately, studies of the early wave of immigration are much more plentiful compared to the post-1965 wave of largely non-European immigrants, so the contemporary situation is an open empirical question. It is likely that the reason for the lack of attention to the current wave (in addition to data collection issues) is that dominant sociological notions about immigration as a crime-facilitating social force have become so taken-for-granted that most researchers do not even consider conducting empirical inquiries into the matter. A strong link between immigration and crime has attained the status of "mythology" among criminologists (Hagan and Palloni, 1999).

In the absence of systematic research, claimsmakers have had free reign to use anecdotal evidence (or no evidence at all) to propagate stereotypes of immigrants as crime-prone. Therefore, by conducting an empirical test of these claims (and the sociological theories that support them) this study can make an important contribution to important popular, policy, and scholarly debates.[16]

CHAPTER 3

Studying Immigration and Homicide

Having located this study within a specific scholarly tradition and a more general public debate in Chapter 2, this chapter describes the research and data collection strategies, along with specific hypotheses, that guide the descriptive patterns and statistical models explored in Chapter 4, as well as the spatial and over-time analyses that follow in Chapter 5.

In 1931 the National Commission on Law Observance and Enforcement (the Wickersham Commission) released an influential multi-volume report on crime that represented the state of the field of crime research at that time. Leading authorities on the subject (e.g., Shaw and McKay, 1931) presented the best-available empirical research on crime and the report is still widely cited. Yet LaFree, Bursik, Short, and Taylor (2000:6-7) note that one report (Report 13, Volume 1) offered a markedly pessimistic review of criminological research, concluding that "nearly all empirical work of that period was characterized by faulty study designs, inappropriate statistical models, bad data, poorly formulated research hypotheses, and/or unwarranted conclusions."

Long-standing debates since the Wickersham reports have generated guidelines for collecting and analyzing high-quality crime data in the most appropriate manner. Drawing on the best insights of this research tradition, my analyses will utilize five strategies in order to generate the most meaningful and valid results. These strategies concern: 1) theoretically informed data disaggregation, 2) the selection of the most appropriate unit of analysis, 3) statistical models based on event counts, 4) qualitative analysis of the spatial distribution of homicide and its structural covariates, and 5) the collection of original data.

Disaggregation

With few exceptions, studies of the structural covariates of violent crime have generated inconsistent results (Land et al., 1990). Basic issues, such as the impact of poverty and inequality on crime rates remain unresolved. Even the study of criminal homicide, the crime for which the most reliable statistics are available, has produced little consensus among researchers about the causal role of key socio-demographic variables. The findings in homicide studies are shaped by the level of analysis (Messner and Tardiff, 1986; but see Parker et al., 1999), model specification issues (e.g., labor market variables attenuate the influence of income, see Crutchfield, 1989), and various data disaggregation strategies (Flewelling and Williams, 1999).

Data disaggregation issues, in particular, have received a great deal of attention in recent years. Scholars have found that different types of homicide (e.g., intimate verses stranger) have distinct causal mechanisms (Avakame, 1998), as do intra- as opposed to inter-ethnic killings (Parker and McCall, 1999). Data disaggregation appears especially important in the area of race/ethnicity and homicide, as a growing body of research has documented (Martinez and Lee, 1999; Hawkins, 1999a). Scholars have begun to move away from generic discussions of "homicide rates" to consider the vastly different homicide patterns displayed by specific racial groups. Unfortunately, due in large part to data collection problems, most research has focused on the black/white racial dichotomy used by the Uniform Crime Reports, at the expense of more finely detailed ethnic comparisons (see Martinez and Lee, 1999). This is a pressing concern given recent challenges to the "racial invariance assumption" (i.e. that structural variables exhibit similar effects across racial groups, see Ousey 1999).

Recall that the major hypothesis guiding this study is that while immigration could potentially elevate race-specific homicide levels in border cities where immigrants settle by increasing the level of macrosocial variables associated with homicide (e.g., economic deprivation, residential instability), it is also possible that the ties immigrants have to their jobs and families are substantial enough to overcome these effects. Therefore, consistent with most prior research on immigration and crime (see Martinez and Lee, 2000b), I expect that the percentage of recent immigrants in a neighborhood will suppress the occurrence of homicide, all other factors being equal. Since the impact of immigration on homicide can be expected to vary by ethnic group, I test this proposition in Chapter 4 using a racially disaggregated data set (see Martinez and Lee, 1999; Hawkins, 1999a; Ousey, 1999).

The Units of Analysis

Parker, McCall, and Land (1999; see also Land et al., 1990) found that studies of the social-structural predictors of homicide continue to generate inconsistent findings across different units of analysis (e.g., states, SMSAs, cities, census tracts). They claim that the unit of analysis per se is not a relevant concern, but rather problems related to research design (e.g., the "partialing fallacy") lead to statistical results that vary across different population aggregations. Their solution is to combine highly correlated independent variables (e.g., poverty, joblessness, and low education rates) into larger indexes (e.g., "the resource deprivation index") which they argue produce stable findings at all levels of analysis. This strategy is fine for some purposes, but it also obscures important variations across local contexts and masks the independent effects of each variable. They note that their approach "prevents researchers from testing competing theories when using highly correlated conceptual measures" (Parker et al., 1999:119).

Since the study proposed here is explicitly interested in the independent effects of recent immigration, which is potentially highly correlated with other independent variables (e.g., poverty), the creation of indexes is not an appropriate strategy. Instead, special attention will be paid to the role of extreme cases, the "partialing fallacy," and other data concerns to insure that the findings are not simply statistical artifacts (see Gordon, 1967; Land, McCall, and Cohen, 1990; Shihadeh and Steffensmeier, 1994; Warner and Rountree, 1997).

There are good theoretical and empirical reasons to dispute the value of indexes, and also the suggestion that the unit of analysis is irrelevant. Travis (1997:1), for example, discovered that although the national homicide rate declined sharply in the 1990s, "not all cities are experiencing this downward trend, and focusing on national trends may mask a complex picture." Therefore, some attention must be paid to the different city contexts in which homicides occur. Yet city-level studies are also not without problems.

Messner and Tardiff (1986) present a compelling theoretical rationale, backed by empirical evidence, that the neighborhood is the most appropriate unit of analysis for testing the effect of structural variables on homicide (see also Osgood, 2000). They point out that large areas such as states or cities are extremely heterogeneous and arbitrarily defined aggregates, and are therefore not meaningful frames of reference. A recent review of city-level studies of the relationship between economic factors and homicide notes that:

> These analyses treat the city as the unit of analysis and do not incorporate within-city variation in the economic factors in question. This approach is not very sensitive, and failure to detect links between homicide and selected economic factors should not be seen as evidence that the links do not exist. In fact, preliminary analyses of within-city variation in economic factors strongly suggest a link to homicide (Travis, 1997:9).

Neighborhoods within cities, roughly approximated by census tracts, are better suited for social comparisons for three reasons.[17] First, they do not contain both urban and rural areas. Second, tracts relate better to the assumed psychological processes by which structural factors generate crime (see Nettler, 1984). And third, judgments of "relative deprivation" more often involve local rather than state-wide or national norms (Messner and Tardiff, 1986). For these reasons, this study will be conducted at the census tract level, with tracts drawn from three distinct city contexts.

In addition to the quantitative tract-level analyses, I will also examine selected tracts more qualitatively in order to compare structural influences on homicide events. I will base this tract-level comparative analysis on maps showing the spatial distribution of high/low homicide areas, high/low immigrant areas, etc., thus reviving a fruitful but currently neglected tradition in the sociology of crime (see Lind, 1930a; 1930b; Shaw and McKay, 1969[1942]). This qualitative assessment will provide an additional check on the quantitative models; the validity of this study therefore relates to the extent to which the qualitative analysis and quantitative models produce similar findings. This dual-methodology design, an enduring contribution of Shaw and McKay's (1969[1942]) classic work, but rare in contemporary homicide studies, is starting to experience a rebirth (cf. Logan and Stults, 1999).

Statistical Models
Poisson Regression

Homicides are distributed across ecological units such as census tracts in a highly skewed manner (Rosenfeld and Decker, 1993; Osgood, 2000) and are not approximately normal in their distribution across urban areas (Kohfeld and Sprague, 1988). Therefore, traditional ordinary least squares (OLS) regression is not an appropriate estimator for such distributions when transformations of the dependent variable (such as logarithmic transformation) do not induce normality. As Osgood (2000) points out, most macrological studies of homicide are at the city or higher level of aggregation (thus assuming that explanatory variables like poverty are invariant across neighborhoods), while existing tract-level studies are invariably based on biased regression coefficients and misleading significance tests.

To accommodate the non-random distribution of homicides, I will employ a maximum likelihood estimator that is designed to deal with counts, in this case, homicide events (Cameron and Trivedi, 1986; Gardner, Mulvey, and Shaw, 1995). Recent developments in the economic and political science literature, along with those emerging in the homicide literature, justifies the use of counts rather than rates (see Balkwell, 1990; Kohfeld and Sprague, 1988). Rates are misleading with respect to the level of homicide in a tract to the degree that persons who are killed in a tract reside in another tract. Using tract population as an independent variable controls for the variation in risk associated with residential population and does not require the untenable assumption that *only* persons who reside in a tract are eligible to be killed there. In addition to this issue, the error terms for tract level homicide rates are likely to be heteroskedastic since tracts with larger populations will exhibit "less fluctuation around true values" than less populous tracts (see Messner and Tardiff, 1986:308; Osgood, 2000).

Specifically, homicides are conceptualized as counts of events per unit of time, a description suggesting that the use of a Poisson random component is most appropriate. In Poisson regression, parameters are estimated through a maximum likelihood procedure which has a number of desirable properties, including an asymptotic distribution, consistency, and efficiency (Fienberg, 1984). Further, the Poisson coefficient divided by its standard error follows a standard t-distribution. Therefore, statistical significance as well as the direction and magnitude of the effect of each independent variable can be assessed (Osgood, 2000). The general analytic strategy is to use Poisson regression to assess the independent effect of theoretically important structural covariates of homicide on race-specific homicide event counts in El Paso, Miami, and San Diego.

Variables

The dependent variables in the group-specific models used in Chapter 4 of this study are black and Latino homicide counts, aggregated to the tract level for the 1985-1995 time period. Table 3.1 presents the variables included in the models, along with their hypothesized relationship to homicide levels. Since the dependent variables are *counts* rather than *rates*, I have included a measure of the black and Latino populations (logged in the Poisson model) to control for the fact that highly populated tracts obviously will have greater numbers of homicide events.[18]

Table 3.1: Hypothesized Relationship of Group-Specific Independent Variables on the Dependent Variables (Group-Specific Census Tract Levels of Homicide).

Independent Variable	Relationship with Dependent Variable
Population	Positive
Instability Index*	Positive
Poverty	Positive
Female-Headed Families	Positive
Male Joblessness	Positive
Young Males	Positive
Spatial Lag	Positive
New Immigrants*	Negative

* Not a group-specific variable

Following tenets of social disorganization theory suggesting that areas with large percentages of vacant buildings and high population turnover will exhibit less effective social control (Shaw and McKay, 1969[1942]), and thus more homicide events, I have constructed a measure that combines these two variables into an "Instability Index." The percentage of vacant buildings was calculated by dividing the number of vacant housing units by the total number of housing units; the population turnover measure is the number of persons who lived in a different housing unit in 1990 than they did five years earlier, divided by the total population. The z-scores of these two measures were then multiplied to create the index.

Next I have included the most widely used opportunity structure variable in homicide studies, the percentage of blacks and Latinos living below the poverty line, as a measure of economic deprivation. In addition, consistent with past research suggesting that family structure influences homicide (Sampson, 1987), I created a variable to account for the percentage of group-specific female-headed families in each tract. This was measured by dividing the number of female-headed families by the total number of families.

Labor market theory (see Crutchfield, 1989; Crutchfield and Pitchford, 1997) argues that a community's job structure will exert an effect on crime beyond that which is captured by economic deprivation measures like poverty. Latino populations in urban neighborhoods are often characterized as the "working poor," while African Americans are thought to have higher levels of joblessness, a distinction difficult to assess at the tract level. Nevertheless, in line with previous research, for both groups I have included the percentage of jobless males, defined as the number of males "not in the labor force" divided by the total number of males, in order to assess the impact of the local labor market on black and Latino homicide events.

I also control for the percentage of black and Latino males that are between the ages of 18 and 24 years, since this age group is commonly thought of as particularly crime-prone. In fact, national studies routinely find that 18-24 year old males have the highest homicide victimization and offending rates (Fox and Zawitz, 2000).

In order to determine the influence of immigration on homicide, I have included a measure of the percent of "new" immigrants (in this case those who arrived in the United States between the years 1980-1990, as measured by the 1990 census). The social and ethnic composition of immigrants to the United States experienced dramatic changes in the last four decades, but as Rumbaut (1996:27) points out, "in its size and above all in its extraordinary diversity, the 1980s has rivaled any other decade in U.S. immigration history." In this context of massive social change, social disorganization theory suggests that the presence of recent immigrants will weaken community organization and institutions, thus affecting criminal activity, by contributing to population turnover and ethnic heterogeneity (Shaw and McKay, 1969[1942]). Furthermore, as I have mentioned, politicians and pundits have suggested that the newest immigrants are a crime-prone group, a claim seized on by the media especially with regard to the 1980 Mariel boatlift in Miami (cf. Lamm and Imhoff, 1985; see also Martinez, 1997 for a discussion).

Unfortunately, there has been no empirical research at the tract level to address these allegations. The current study is therefore the first to assess the impact of recent immigration, independent of variables like poverty and age structure, on homicide events. Despite the widespread assumption that new immigrants generate higher crime rates, I argue that immigrants may stabilize communities due to ties to family and work and thus suppress homicide levels (see Martinez and Lee, 2000a; Martinez and Lee, 2000b; Portes and Stepick, 1993).

One must be cautious of grouping together such diverse groups of people into a class labeled as "new immigrants," given the great variation apparent in these groups in ethnicity, social class, circumstances of immigration, and manner of reception in the United States. Unfortunately, finer distinctions cannot be made with tract-level data available for the Poisson models, due to the small city-wide numbers (of Asians, for example) and the lack of detail in the census data regarding the year of entry of specific groups. Chapter 5 presents a qualitative analysis of the spatial distribution of demographic characteristics and homicide victimization levels of these individual groups in order to partially address this concern.

On the other hand, a careful discussion of "new immigrants" as a single group in the statistical models can be justified for two reasons. First, both popular stereotypes and sociological theories tend not to make distinctions among specific groups regarding the alleged positive relationship of "new immigrants" with crime rates (cf. Lamm and Imhoff, 1985; Shaw and McKay, 1969[1942]). An empirical test of these claims, as they have been constructed, would be useful.

Second, regardless of ethnicity (e.g., Haitian, Jamaican, Mariel Cuban, Mexican, Asian) the most recent immigrants have tended to settle in the most disadvantaged areas of the three cities investigated in this study, and all have experienced varying degrees of prejudice and discrimination (Martinez and Lee, 2000a; Martinez and Lee, 2000b; Simon, 1987; Zinsmeister, 1987; Portes and Stepick, 1985). In the past, the most recent groups of immigrants have been briefly associated with high crime rates in some (but not all) cities, again regardless of ethnicity (Shaw and McKay, 1969[1942]), but this general association has not been tested for the immigrant groups that have arrived in the last four decades. Indeed, at one point in their classic study, Shaw and McKay (1969[1942]:153) felt justified in combining American-born blacks with various immigrant groups for purposes of analysis because:

> Both categories... refer to groups of low economic status, making their adjustment to a complex urban environment.... and will therefore be considered together, in order to study [the] segregation of newer arrivals, on a city wide scale.

Although I do not combine blacks and immigrants in this study, grouping together recent immigrant groups seems reasonable as an initial step in the investigation of the immigration/crime linkage. Future statistical studies will hopefully be able to pursue the disaggregation strategy to a greater extent.

Finally, researchers have increasingly recognized the importance of external contingencies and spatial relationships on a given community's level of crime and violence (for a review, see Anselin, Cohen, Cook, Gorr, and Tita, 2000). This recognition has been most closely associated with a reformulation of the social disorganization perspective that now encompasses private, parochial, and public levels of social control (Bursik and Grasmick, 1993). According to this view, even a stable, "organized," neighborhood may exhibit high rates of crime due to its proximity to other "disorganized" and/or high-crime areas (see Heitgerd and Bursik, 1987). The impact on homicide of internal levels of variables such as poverty and neighborhood "instability," while still important, may be mediated by processes external to a given tract. Thus, a variable like poverty may not have the uniform effect on a tract's level of violence as theory would predict. Consistent with this line of work, I included a spatial autocorrelation term (i.e., "spatial lag") in order to capture the effect of surrounding tracts' homicide levels on a given tract's level.

Spatial autocorrelation in this study refers to nonrandom clustering in homicides that is not a function of the explanatory variables in the model. Such clustering may result from diffusion or spillover processes in which high rates of violence in one community result in increases in adjacent or nearby communities (Anselin et al., 2000). Alternatively, negative spatial autocorrelation, in which high homicide counts in a tract are associated with low counts in nearby tracts, might result from enforcement activity or other conditions that displace crimes across neighborhood boundaries. In other words, because a given tract's homicide level may be influenced by processes external to tract boundaries, researchers must statistically control for these processes or risk incorrectly attributing their effects to internal conditions, such as tract-specific levels of poverty or immigration (see Cliff and Ord, 1981 for the classic discussion of spatial autocorrelation models).

While attempts to model external effects represent a relatively recent development in the criminological literature, Land and Deane (1992) offer an accepted strategy. I follow their advice to model spatial autocorrelation in two stages. In the first stage, a "spatially lagged dependent variable" (Land and Deane 1992:237) was created by obtaining the fitted values of the dependent variable (homicide) from a Poisson (or negative binomial) regression on the independent variables. These fitted values were transformed into a spatial lag variable, which was then included with the independent variables in a second-stage regression. The results from the second-stage models are reported in the analysis in Chapter 4.

The procedure I used for creating the spatial lag term was as follows. First, in the computer program *SpaceStat* (Anselin, 1995), I created a distance matrix based on tract centroid coordinates and then merged the file containing this variable with a file containing the fitted values of the dependent variable that I created in *Limdep version 7.0*.

Second, I transformed the distance matrix to an inverse distance weights matrix (no limits were imposed so that all tracts received a weight based on their distance). Third, I row standardized the inverse distance weights matrix to adjust each weight so that values across a row summed to one. Finally, I created a spatial lag average using the fitted values of tract-levels of black and Latino homicide and exported this variable back into *Limdep* for inclusion in the regression models.

Qualitative Analysis

In Chapter 5, I use a qualitative method to explore the patterns generated by the statistical models in more detail. Specifically, I conduct spatial analyses of tract-level homicide patterns using maps generated with *Arcview* GIS computer software. One advantage of this methodology is the ability to explore the patterns of specific groups (e.g., Asians in San Diego) that cannot be assessed through statistical models because of insufficient numbers. Another plus is that a small number of tracts within a particular city can be compared along selected characteristics (e.g., poverty, new immigrants). The visual presentation of this material is enhanced by the use of maps, which give the reader a sense of location, as opposed to simply listing numbers in tabular format.

Shaw and McKay (1969[1942]) demonstrated the value of maps in their classic study of delinquency in Chicago, and later in cities such as Philadelphia, Boston, and Cleveland. Some of the most compelling evidence we have that delinquency is not vitally related to race/ethnicity is found in Shaw and McKay's maps. This kind of research was prominent in pre-WWII era crime studies (see Lind, 1930a; 1930b; Hayner, 1937; Short, 1969:xxvii), but has declined since then (but see Logan and Stults, 1999; Morenoff and Sampson, 1997).

Inspired by Shaw and McKay, and others from the Chicago School, Andrew Lind (1930a; 1930b) used maps and other methods to investigate the differences of homogeneous but poor "ghettos" compared to heterogeneous, disorganized, and poor "slums." According to Lind's view, crime might flourish in slums but not in ghettos, even though both are characterized by economic deprivation and other deleterious social conditions, because ghetto residents exert a degree of control over neighbors that is missing in disorganized slums (Lind, 1930b).[19] He argued that the "social atmosphere" was markedly different in ghettos and slums:

One [the ghetto] breathes of warmth, intimacy, color; the other of anonymity, chilling distances, drabness. In the one life is on the plane of close, compelling, family and neighborhood disciplines and in the other of impersonal relationships and private convenience (Lind, 1930b:208).

As an example, Lind discussed patterns of Japanese delinquency in two neighborhoods in Honolulu, Hawaii. One, an exclusively Japanese community, exhibited a "complete absence of juvenile delinquency" (Lind, 1930b:209). The other, an ethnically heterogeneous area, was characterized a high level of delinquency for all groups living there, including the Japanese. While this study was not able to statistically control for other community influences on delinquency (given the methodological shortcomings of the time), it was able to demonstrate the merit of studying the contrasting patterns found in specific neighborhoods.

The current study builds on this qualitative tradition, but also has the advantage of using statistical models to uncover the independent effects of particular community features on homicide. Once the most important structural covariates of homicide are isolated in this manner, I use maps to compare and contrast characteristics of areas in which immigrant groups have settled in order to ascertain which factors affect particular groups. For example, do the characteristics of predominantly Asian areas in San Diego with high Asian homicide rates differ from those with low Asian rates? If poverty is a statistically significant predictor of Latino homicide events in the Poisson models, do the maps show any variation in poverty levels in areas with high Latino homicide levels and in which new immigrant groups have settled?

These questions cannot be answered without an examination of spatial distributions. Furthermore, showing the location of high homicide tracts may assist future efforts using ethnographic methods to uncover differences in "social atmosphere" that are obscured by statistical models (see Lind, 1930b). Finally, the qualitative evidence I present can substantiate the validity of the statistical findings as well as point out the limitations of exclusively quantitative research.

Data Collection

Regardless of the sophistication of its statistical and analytical models, research results and conclusions are only as good as the data on which they are constructed. Therefore, in order to contrast the macrological conditions influencing race-specific homicide events in three border cities, original data have been gathered on all homicides that occurred during 1985-1995 directly from the homicide investigations unit of the Miami and San Diego police departments, and up to 1994 in El Paso.[20] This study is part of a larger project that collected all available information on the 3,356 homicides known to police in these cities during this time period (435 in El Paso, 1,548 homicides in Miami, and 1,497 in San Diego). Direct access to detailed internal files has allowed me to distinguish Latinos from other ethnic groups, something that is not fully possible with the FBI's Uniform Crime Reports (in the internal files Latinos are designated with an "L" in Miami and an "M," for "Mexican," in El Paso and San Diego). In fact, most widely available, existing data sets are useless for the purposes of this study (e.g., crime surveys do not capture homicides, while race-specific homicide data sets that include groups like Latinos are rare).

In addition to these advantages, collecting original data is important for pragmatic reasons as well. While police files are subject to various institutional practices that filter reality in systematic ways, and thus are not "unbiased" reflections of homicide events (see Smith, 1974), this is as close as a researcher can get to actually observing large numbers of these rare events. Despite being somewhat removed from the event itself, the researcher does have a measure of control over the coding and cleaning of these data that is absent when pre-existing data sets are used. This is especially relevant when the ethnicity of participants in an incident is a central concern, since multiple sources of information can be used to assess the accuracy of the ethnicity recorded by police detectives. For example, in Miami a few Latinos were mistakenly coded as "white" in the files, but other information such as their surnames and country of birth allowed them to be identified and re-coded as "Latino." Thus, even if the police designations of ethnicity were forwarded to the FBI, because of coding errors the Uniform Crime Reports might still not present an accurate picture of victim and offender ethnicity.

Equally important for the present analysis, the street address of the occurrence of each homicide incident is contained in the police files, which enabled the mapping of the spatial distribution of homicide events in each city and allowed each case to be linked to data from the 1990

decennial census. Thus, the units of analysis for this study
are the 352 census tracts with more than 500 residents in
the three cities: 86 of which are in El Paso, 70 are in
Miami, and 196 are in San Diego.

Research Setting: Immigration in Three Border Cities

Before concluding this chapter, I briefly describe the local
history of immigration in the three cities that serve as the
research setting for this study. As mentioned in Chapter 1
(Endnote 1), San Diego, El Paso, and Miami ranked first,
second, and nineteenth, respectively, in immigrant
admissions to the United States in 1986, relative to all other
points of entry, according to figures compiled by the
Immigration and Naturalization Service (1987). These
cities can therefore be considered on the "border" because
they serves as major ports of entry and final destinations for
immigrants, even if they are not physically located next to
foreign country, as in the case of Miami.

Before I turn to a discussion of each city's local
context, it is important to highlight the national trends that
have affected the three cities, as all have been substantially
transformed in recent decades by the arrival of newcomers
from abroad. While previous waves of immigrants
"provided the cheap labor force essential to
industrialization and expansion in America" (Pedraza,
1996a:2), the most recent wave (largely Latino and Asian)
has encountered "an increasingly post-industrial, service-
oriented society." This has important implications because
sociological theories of immigrant crime were developed
using data on earlier waves of European immigrants to
Northeast and Midwest cities with industrial economies.
The context is quite different in the three Sunbelt cities,
both in terms of population characteristics and the nature of
the labor market. Scholars have demonstrated that
immigrants do not simply seek out existing jobs, but in

many cases they "fill occupational niches that would not exist in their absence" (Linton, 2002:58). The "enclave economy" created by Cuban immigrants, which transformed the city of Miami, is a classic example (Portes and Stepick, 1993).

In terms of population demographics, Rumbaut (1992) notes that the 1980 Census reported that among the foreign-born, 87.4% of Asians, 68.6% of Mexicans, 87.2% of Cubans, and 95.4% of Haitians entered the U.S. between 1960 and 1980. These groups have had the most significant impact on the three cities and their immigration and settlement patterns continued to impact each city's structural characteristics throughout the period examined in this book (i.e., 1980-1995). Immigration in the 1980s surpassed any previous decade in U.S. history, and legal admission records were set in both 1990 and 1991 (Rumbaut, 1996). By 1990, over 80 percent of immigrants originated in Latin America and Asia, a fact with important implications for the three cities (Pedraza, 1996a). For example, at the county level, each local area experienced considerable growth in the local Latino population between 1980 and 1990. The increase was highest in San Diego County (85.6%), followed by Dade County (Miami; 64.1%), and El Paso County (38.6%, see Rumbaut, 1992).

El Paso

Recent immigration to El Paso is principally from Mexico, but it is important to mention that Mexicans have dominated the population of that city since its founding four hundred years ago (Suro, 1998). For example, according to figures from the 1990 census, Mexicans comprised 69% of the city's total population (Martinez, 2002). Yet the economic benefits of being in a numerical majority in this city, as with much of the Southwest, have often been lacking. The historical context is informative in this regard. Pedraza (1996a:2) described the situation facing Mexicans in southwestern states such as Texas and California following the war between the U.S. and Mexico as one of "extreme racial prejudice" and "castlike subordination."

It is not surprising, then, that El Paso would experience the formation of "barrios," such as Chihuahuita, where relatively poor Latinos have self-segregated (or been forced by social disadvantage) and avoided contact with the city's white residents. Such isolation has had severe consequences for native-born and immigrant Mexicans in El Paso's barrios, where, for example, 71% of Chihuahuita's residents had incomes below the federal poverty line in 1990 (Martinez, 2002). It was in this barrio that the distinctive "zoot-suit" subculture of the 1920s and 1930s first developed and later spread to other parts of the southwest, ultimately to be used by law enforcement and the media to create the stereotype of the "violent Mexican" (Escobar, 1999). Such images persist today, as recent initiatives designed to "protect" the U.S. border in El Paso (and also San Diego) have been justified, in part, on myths about crime-prone immigrants (Nevins, 2002).

Mexican immigrants, such as those who settle in El Paso, remain among the lowest in terms of socio-economic status relative to other Latino groups, such as Cubans in Miami. For example, among the foreign-born living in the U.S. in 1980, only 3% of Mexicans had graduated college and only 5.4% had "upper white collar" occupations (Rumbaut, 1992). Similar figures for Cubans were 17.1% and 19.3%. Thus, the social context of immigration in El Paso is quite different than in Miami, and sociological theories would suggest that the arrival of relatively impoverished Mexican immigrants should increase homicide levels in the El Paso neighborhoods in which they settle.

Miami

As mentioned above, Cubans in Miami tend to more economically well-off than other Latino groups. This due to the large number of middle-class Cubans who fled communist Cuba in the 1960s and benefited from the 1961 Cuban Refugee Program that provided a number of material advantages rarely afforded to immigrant groups, including financial assistance, job training, and education (Garcia, 1996). According to national figures from the 1990 census, Cubans had the highest mean family income of all Latino groups and they participated in white collar occupations at a level comparable to the general population of the U.S. – the only Latino group in that situation (Rumbaut, 1992).

Yet Cubans in Miami are a diverse group, and not all have experienced the good fortune of the first arrivals, especially the 125,000 refugees who left Cuba through the harbor of Mariel and arrived in southern Florida in 1980 (Portes and Stepick, 1993). These "Marielitos" faced a much more hostile reception than those who arrived in the 1960s, and they quickly became targets for stereotypes and discrimination. In the popular imagination, the newly arrived Cubans were likely to be criminals, including "large group of very, very violent [Mariels], a lot of psychopaths" (Lamm and Imhoff, 1985:67). If these claims were true, we would expect that Cuban immigrants who arrived during the time period captured by the current study would increase levels of homicide in the parts of Miami where they established residence.

In addition to Cuban immigrants, Miami has experienced sustained immigration from Central America and the Caribbean. One consequence is that the Greater Miami area now has the largest foreign-born population in the U.S. (Grenier and Perez, 1996). Haitians, for example, began arriving in formidable numbers in the late 1970s, and especially in the 1980s, and now comprise the largest non-Cuban immigrant group (Dunn, 1997). As with the Mariels, Haitians were not well-received, greeted with government assistance, or readily incorporated into the local economy. They too faced prejudice and discrimination, resulting in social and economic marginalization (Stepick, 1998). The fact that many undocumented Haitain refugees who arrived from "the least developed nation in the Western Hemisphere" spoke little English also contributed to this marginalization (Grenier and Perez, 1996:371). It is therefore reasonable to expect that Haitian neighborhoods may exhibit inflated levels of homicide relative to other parts of the city. However, some authors have noted the tendency of Afro-Caribbean groups to fare better economically than native-born blacks (see James, 2002). If true for Haitians in Miami, this might mitigate the effects of discrimination and impact their involvement in homicide.

San Diego

Unlike El Paso and Miami, native-born whites remain the most populous group in San Diego. But Mexicans have maintained a strong presence throughout the city's history. By 1990, census figures indicated that Mexicans comprised 20% of San Diego's citywide population, with some neighborhoods approaching 80% (Martinez, 2002). As with California more generally, San Diego's Mexican population increased drastically because of the Bracero program – a World War II policy designed to import cheap immigrant labor to deal with the domestic labor shortage caused by the war, particularly in the agricultural sector (Romo, 1996; Rumbaut, 1992).

In addition to a steady stream of arrivals from Mexico, San Diego has also experienced substantial immigration from Asia, especially since the 1965 Immigration Act allowed Asians to enter the U.S. under family reunification provisions and occupational preferences. The latter encouraged immigration among highly educated and well-trained Asian professionals. For example, in 1964 on 14 percent of immigrant scientists and engineers came to the U.S. from Asia. By 1970, the number climbed to 62 percent (Ong and Liu, 1994). San Diego certainly has its share of Asian professionals. But Asians in this city are a diverse lot, including a relatively recent wave of less educated and impoverished arrivals from Vietnam, a large middle class contingent of Filipinos employed by the U.S. Navy, and refugees from Laos and Cambodia (Carino, 1996; Ong and Liu, 1994). Espiritu (1995:24) cites census figures reporting almost 96,000 Filipinos in San Diego County, and although "increasing geographical dispersion of the community is and obstacle to its cohesion," there are still a large number of newly arrived professionals settling in affluent areas of the city. While we may expect that the presence of such immigrants should suppress homicide (see also T. Waters 1999:58), the impact of other impoverished Asian immigrant groups, as well as newcomers from Mexico, remains an empirical question.

In sum, the immigration patterns in these three cities exhibit important variations. El Paso has received immigrants primarily from Mexico. Cubans, Afro-Caribbeans, and other Latin American groups have immigrated in large numbers to Miami. And San Diego has had sustained waves of Mexican and Asian immigration. This raises a fundamental question regarding the extent to which the different immigration histories determine neighborhood levels of homicide in each city, independent of basic social conditions (e.g., poverty, joblessness). In other words, do local conditions – of which immigrant flows are a major part – play a key role in urban violence, or is this outcome shaped by the same social forces across city contexts? These three cities represent strategic sites to begin to address such concerns.

Conclusion

This chapter has reviewed the guidelines that shaped the ways in which data were collected and analyzed in this study. Drawing on past research, I have concluded that five strategies will generate the most meaningful and valid results. First, data disaggregation by race/ethnicity is warranted. Second, the most appropriate unit of analysis for this study is census tracts within distinct cities. Third, statistical models based on event counts (Poisson regression) represent an improvement over previous studies which rely on OLS regression. Fourth, qualitative analysis of the spatial distribution of homicide and its structural covariates (i.e., maps in the tradition of Shaw and McKay, 1969[1942] and Lind, 1930a) can provide a check on the validity of the statistical analyses as well as explore issues that quantitative methods cannot address.

The fifth and final guideline is that the collection of original data directly from police files is essential in order to implement the first four strategies. Racial disaggregation in cities with large Latino populations is not possible with existing data sets. Collecting original data allows individual cases to be matched with tract-level attributes, thus providing the event counts that are needed for Poisson regression. And finally, since the police files contain the address of the incident, maps of the spatial distribution of homicide can be constructed.

CHAPTER 4

The Independent Effects
of Immigration on Homicide

This chapter describes both the prevalence of homicide and the social/demographic context of El Paso, Miami, and San Diego. It then presents a multivariate test of the independent variables that were identified as important predictors of homicide in the previous chapter.

Homicide in El Paso, Miami, and San Diego

For the purposes of this study, a key part of a city's local context is its level of homicide. After all, the differences observed in the homicide involvement of specific ethnic groups as victims or offenders is partly dependent on whether a given group settles in a more or less violent city. For example, Lee, Martinez, and Rodriguez (2000) found that the homicide rates of specific immigrant groups (e.g., Cubans or Mexicans) were related to the pre-existing level of homicide in the cities to which they immigrated.

As Table 4.1 shows, the three cities examined in this study display markedly different total and group-specific homicide victimization rates for the 1985-1995 time period. While the total rates for El Paso and San Diego are well below national averages for cities of a similar size, Miami's rates are almost double that of its national reference group. Much of Miami's disparity with national rates can be attributed to its exceedingly high black homicide rate

(82.00 per 100,000), while its Latino and Anglo rates (25.54 and 25.05, respectively) are virtually identical and just slightly above the national average (20.41). El Paso's black rate (17.98) is the highest of that city's ethnic groups (Latinos: 7.69; Anglos: 1.65), but still below its national comparison group (21.55). As in the other two cities, San Diego's black rate (34.82) is higher than its Latino or Anglo rate (21.68 and 5.69, respectively).

Table 4.1: Homicide Rates Per 100,000 by City, 1985-1995.

	El Paso	Miami	San Diego
National Average*	21.55	20.41	27.70
Total	7.80	36.49	11.44
Black	17.98	82.00	34.82
Latino	7.69	25.54	21.68
Anglo	1.65	25.05	5.69

* Total rate for cities of similar size (source: Fox and Zawitz, 2000); El Paso rates are for 1985-1994.

Note that homicide levels cannot be attributed to race or city context alone, but vary according to the interaction of these two factors. For example, while blacks had the highest homicide rates within each city, the black rate in El Paso was lower than the rates of blacks, Latinos, and Anglos in Miami, and lower than all but Anglos in San

Diego. Similarly, Anglos in Miami had a higher homicide rate than all groups in El Paso, and all but blacks in San Diego.

These variations imply that the effects of the independent variables on homicide in the multivariate analyses discussed in this chapter might be shaped by features of each city's context that are not measured in the statistical models (e.g., changing levels of gun ownership, gang or drug activity, or a local "subculture" of violence). For example, the effect of poverty on homicide may be mediated to some extent by a given city's volume of "retaliation" killings, such that poverty may be less important in a city where a large number of retaliation killings cross census tract boundaries and drive up levels in less poor neighborhoods, compared with a city where this occurs infrequently. While the present study does not test this kind of hypothesis, the results must be interpreted cautiously, since factors other than those investigated here might be influencing homicide in the El Paso, Miami, and San Diego.

Descriptive Statistics

Table 4.2 presents descriptive statistics for the variables used in the Poisson models that comprise the quantitative analysis for this study. As with the previous discussion of homicide and immigration rates, the levels of each variable differ (sometimes greatly) among the three cities.

Looking first at the dependent variables in Table 4.2, it is clear that Miami has a much higher average tract-level count of black and Latino homicides than either El Paso or San Diego. This is consistent with Miami's much higher homicide rates reported above. El Paso has the lowest count of black homicides (.29), San Diego has 1.95, and Miami has 9.79. Although rates are not used in the Poisson

Table 4.2: Descriptive Statistics for the Regression Models

	El Paso Mean (SD)	Miami Mean (SD)	San Diego Mean (SD)
Black Homicides	.29	9.79	1.95
	(.59)	(16.29)	(4.95)
Annualized Rate			
(per 1,000)	.16	.71	.37
Latino Homicides	2.88	8.53	2.78
	(2.84)	(6.88)	(6.23)
Annualized Rate			
(per 1,000)	.07	.24	.22
Non-Latino Blacks	187	1259	486
	(215)	(1714)	(851)
Latinos	4130	3179	1127
	(2346)	(2527)	(1399)
Instability	-.701	.513	.124
Index	(1.29)	(2.03)	(1.48)
% Poverty			
Black	18.72	38.96	15.80
	(25.73)	(21.87)	(19.42)
Latino	29.78	31.95	17.25
	(16.77)	(16.01)	(12.89)
% Female-Headed Families			
Black	19.88	37.01	24.56
	(26.87)	(30.82)	(31.11)
Latino	22.54	29.23	19.88
	(9.23)	(20.71)	(19.08)
Tract N	86	70	196

Table 4.2: Descriptive Statistics, Continued

	El Paso Mean (SD)	Miami Mean (SD)	San Diego Mean (SD)
% Male Joblessness			
Black	28.98 (28.48)	33.91 (23.89)	18.18 (20.36)
Latino	25.89 (10.43)	29.13 (16.40)	19.08 (13.57)
% Young and Male			
Black	8.53 (9.68)	5.27 (5.61)	9.29 (11.00)
Latino	9.14 (2.55)	6.33 (2.86)	10.48 (6.37)
% New Immigrants	8.74 (5.80)	26.63 (14.36)	9.62 (8.70)
Spatial Lag			
Black	.29 (.06)	9.40 (3.44)	2.13 (.85)
Latino	3.00 (.48)	8.81 (.96)	2.89 (1.12)
Tract N	86	70	196

Note: The homicide values are the tract means for 1985-1995 in Miami and San Diego and 1985-1994 in El Paso. All other variables (except spatial lags) are from the 1990 census.

regression models, Table 4.2 also presents tract-level black and Latino homicide rates (per 1,000 residents). Looking at this variable, Miami's rate (.71) is more than double that of San Diego (.37), and more than four times higher than El Paso's rate (.16).

In terms of Latino homicide events, San Diego has the lowest average (2.78), El Paso has a similar number (2.88), while Miami is again much higher (8.53). More informative are the tract-level homicide rates. Unlike the picture that emerged for black homicide at the tract level, Latino homicide rates are roughly similar in Miami (.24) and San Diego (.22), both of which are more than three times the rate in El Paso (.07).

Table 4.2 next includes the population counts for blacks and Latinos. This variable controls for homicide risk, since a greater number of people are likely to generate increased numbers of homicide events. On average, Miami has more black residents per tract (1259), and El Paso more Latino residents (4130), than the other cities. Note that there are relatively few blacks on average in El Paso (187) and San Diego (486).

As discussed above, the instability index was constructed to indicate a tract's "social disorganization." Recall that this index combines the percent of vacant buildings and the percent of occupants who lived in a different housing unit in 1990 than they did five years earlier. Table 4.2 shows that Miami (5.13) has a much higher level of "instability" than El Paso (-.701) or San Diego (1.24).

The poverty measure yielded some especially interesting findings. First, Miami has higher levels of poverty on average for both blacks and Latinos than the other cities, though Latinos in Miami and El Paso are quite comparable (31.95% and 29.78% below the poverty line, respectively). Second, note that Latinos in El Paso and San Diego exhibited higher levels of poverty than blacks. El

Paso's Latino poverty rate (29.78%) is much higher than its black poverty rate (18.72%), which may have implications for the effect of poverty on group-specific homicides, particularly in this city.

In keeping with the trends for the other variables discussed so far, Miami has higher levels of female headed families than the other cities, for both blacks and Latinos. The percentage of black female-headed families in Miami (37.01%) is the highest for all groups (Latinos in Miami were second with 29.23%). This pattern continues for male joblessness; Miami has the highest percentage for both blacks and Latinos (33.91% and 29.13%, respectively), although El Paso's male joblessness levels are also relatively high.

Up to this point, Miami has exhibited the highest levels of structural characteristics widely thought to be related to increased homicide, which may partly account for this city's high homicide rates at both the city and tract levels, as shown in Tables 4.1 and 4.2. However, Miami has smaller percentages of males aged 18-24 than the other cities (San Diego has the highest levels: 9.29% young black males and 10.48% young Latino males). Although Miami's comparatively high homicide rates cannot be explained by an unusually large young male population, this variable could influence homicide within each city in the expected manner, independent of the effects of the other variables included in the models, and is included as a control.

Next, Table 4.2 presents the percentage of "new immigrants" (i.e., those who arrived between 1980 and 1990) in each city. Miami has the highest proportion of new immigrants (26.63%), about three times higher than either El Paso (8.74%) or San Diego (9.62%). Although Miami has both the highest homicide and immigration rates of the three cities, we must be careful not to conclude that recent immigration caused homicide because immigrants are not evenly distributed across the cities. Rather, they tend to settle in segregated areas, so we must model the effects of recent immigration (independent of other structural covariates of homicide) at the tract level before a definitive conclusion can be drawn.

Finally, Table 4.2 includes the means and standard deviations for the spatial lag variables. As we would logically expect, these variables mirror the trends present in the group-specific homicide counts for each city.

Correlations

Tables 4.3 and 4.4 present bivariate correlations for the variables used in the Poisson models. Following the strategy pursued in Lee, Martinez, and Rosenfeld (2001), I present correlations for combined Latino and black models. In other words, all three cities are combined in each group-specific Table. [Correlation matrices for all six individual models can be found in M. T. Lee, 2000]. Correlations, of course, are less useful than the coefficients produced by the method of Poisson regression, because regression controls for the effects of other variables.

But correlations are valuable for alerting researchers to potential collinearity problems in regression models. Including highly correlated (e.g., r=.80, see Warner and Roundtree, 1997; Shihadeh and Steffensmeier, 1994) independent variables in the same model can lead to a host of problems (e.g., the "partialing fallacy," see Land et al., 1990; Gordon, 1967). Therefore, when correlations are high additional diagnostics must be performed to ensure that results are not merely statistical artifacts. Fortunately, none of the correlations in Table 4.3 and 4.4 are above .80 (one potential collinearity issue in the El Paso Latino model is discussed in the next section).

Table 4.3: Correlations for the Combined Latino Model

	1	2	3	4	5	6	7	8
1. Latino Homicide								
2. (Ln) Latino Population	.44							
3. Instability Index	.07	-.17						
4. Latino Poverty	.45	.34	.26					
5. Latino Female-Headed Family	.15	.09	.17	.47				
6. Latino Male Joblessness	.20	.19	.09	.38	.25			
7. Young Latino Males	-.05	.05	-.08	.01	-.00	.11		
8. New Immigrants	.59	.47	.12	.43	.14	.19	-.05	
9. Latino Spatial Lag	.55	.29	.21	.39	.21	.28	-.24	.70

Table 4.4: Correlations for the Combined Black Model

	1	2	3	4	5	6	7	8
1. Black Homicide								
2. (Ln) Black Population	.46							
3. Instability Index	.31	.18						
4. Black Poverty	.31	.09	.19					
5. Blk Female-Headed Family	.36	.48	.16	.31				
6. Black Male Joblessness	.19	.14	.02	.18	.19			
7. Young Black Males	-.02	.17	.01	-.11	.09	.13		
8. New Immigrants	.10	.04	.12	.37	.22	.19	-.12	
9. Black Spatial Lag	.59	.32	.30	.39	.31	.16	-.10	.49

Poisson and Negative Binomial Results
Latino Models

Consider first the Latino-specific models presented in Table 4.5. Other than the expected effects for tract population, the only variable with significant effects (at the .01 level) on Latino homicide victimization across all three cities is the poverty rate. Higher levels of poverty are strongly associated with higher levels of homicide. The spatial lag variable is also consistently related to homicide, although only at the .05 level in El Paso and Miami. Specifically, I found that Latino homicide in a given tract is positively related to the characteristics of surrounding tracts, suggesting that a process of diffusion may be at work (Anselin et al. 2000). The instability index is significantly associated with homicide in El Paso and San Diego, with less stable neighborhoods exhibiting higher levels of homicide. The percentage of female-headed families is significantly related to homicide in Miami and San Diego; contrary to expectation, the relationship is negative. Communities with a higher fraction of female-headed families have lower levels of homicide. Neither male joblessness nor the young male measure are linked to homicide levels in the three cities. Finally, net of other influences, the percentage of recent immigrants in the neighborhood is significantly associated with Latino homicide levels only in El Paso, where the direction of this effect is negative.

In sum, the results for the Latino models differ somewhat across the three cities. The only substantively important effect that was consistently significant at the .01 level is for poverty. High poverty rates are associated with higher levels of Latino homicide. The lack of a positive relationship between recent immigration and Latino homicide was also uniform; the two were unrelated in two cities and negatively related in El Paso. Other results are

Table 4.5: Poisson or Negative Binomial Regression Results (Latino Models)

	El Paso	Miami[b]	San Diego[b]
Intercept	-9.37**	-2.29**	-5.44**
	(1.47)	(.792)	(.953)
(Ln) Population[a]	2.26**	.762**	1.32**
	(.338)	(.170)	(.408)
Instability Index	.119*	.002	.152*
	(.069)	(.036)	(.085)
% Poverty[a]	.015**	.032**	.036**
	(.008)	(.007)	(.011)
% Female-Headed Families[a]	.010	-.012**	-.015*
	(.013)	(.005)	(.009)
% Male Joblessness[a]	.020	-.003	.005
	(.013)	(.006)	(.010)
% Young and Male[a]	-.003	-.040	-.008
	(.036)	(.033)	(.023)
% New Immigrants	-.046**	.000	-.007
	(.024)	(.006)	(.019)
Spatial Lag[a]	.483*	.171*	.514**
	(.266)	(.095)	(.126)
Log-Likelihood	-153.66**	-190.00**	-297.31**
(N)	(86)	(70)	(196)

Note: Standard Errors are in parentheses.
[a] Group-Specific Data
[b] Negative Binomial Model
* p<.05 ** p<.01 (one-tailed)

less consistent. One possible interpretation is the presence of multicollinearity in the models, which would produce inflated standard errors and instability in the parameter estimates. Inspection of the city-specific correlation matrices (see M. T. Lee, 2000) and diagnostics for the Latino models indicates the presence of collinearity in the El Paso model involving the measure of female-headed families and the poverty rate ($r = .73$) and also between the new immigration variable and poverty ($r = .79$). An examination of the variance inflation factors (VIFs) indicated that the poverty variable was the potential problem (i.e., VIF > 4). I therefore reestimated the El Paso equation with the poverty rate removed. The only difference in results is that the coefficient for the female-headed family measure becomes significant in the model without the poverty rate. There are no indications of multicollinearity in the other models.

The inconsistent results across the cities, therefore, do not appear to be due to instabilities induced by the correlations among the regressors. In any event, I found no inconsistency for the construct of greatest interest, the percentage of recent immigrants. Thus, immigration is not related to higher Latino homicide levels in these three cities.

Black Models

The results for the black-specific models are displayed in Table 4.6. Here I found that the population variable is significant in Miami and San Diego. The lack of relationship for this measure of homicide risk in El Paso is due to unique characteristics of the black population in this city, a subject I address below. The instability index is related to black homicide levels in El Paso and San Diego, suggesting that blacks are less likely to be homicide victims in more stable neighborhoods.

Table 4.6: Poisson or Negative Binomial Regression Results (Black Models)

	El Paso	Miami[b]	San Diego[b]
Intercept	-3.83**	-2.27**	-7.03**
	(1.47)	(.647)	(.420)
(Ln) Population[a]	.832	1.07**	1.95**
	(.557)	(.165)	(.145)
Instability Index	.291*	.057	.368**
	(.169)	(.049)	(.065)
% Poverty[a]	-.000	.014**	.013**
	(.011)	(.007)	(.005)
% Female-Headed Families[a]	.002	.001	-.006**
	(.008)	(.006)	(.003)
% Male Joblessness[a]	.022**	.009*	.023**
	(.010)	(.006)	(.004)
% Young and Male[a]	-.030	.024	-.015
	(.030)	(.023)	(.011)
% New Immigrants	-.040	-.025**	.015**
	(.052)	(.007)	(.007)
Spatial Lag[a]	2.38	.055	.492**
	(4.03)	(.046)	(.109)
Log-Likelihood	-50.52**	-152.83**	-205.11**
(N)	(86)	(70)	(196)

Note: Standard Errors are in parentheses.
[a] Group-Specific Data
[b] Negative Binomial Model
* $p < .05$ ** $p < .01$ (one-tailed)

Unlike the Latino models, the poverty rate is associated with black homicide in the expected positive direction in only two of the three cities (Miami and San Diego), although male joblessness is consistently related to higher homicide levels. As with the Latino models, the female-headed family measure does not exhibit the positive relationship with black homicide predicted by the literature; it is negative and significant in San Diego and null in Miami and El Paso. The spatial lag term is significant only in San Diego. In other words, controlling for other influences, San Diego neighborhoods where black homicide risk is high tend to be located close to neighborhoods where it is also high. Finally, the immigration measure is negatively related to black homicide levels in Miami, positively related to black homicide in San Diego neighborhoods, and null in El Paso. Inspection of the correlation matrices and regression diagnostics revealed no multicollinearity in the black-specific models.

Discussion and Implications of the Statistical Findings

A simultaneous examination of Tables 4.5 and 4.6 reveals a great deal of variation by race and place in the factors that shape group-specific homicide counts within urban communities on the border, suggesting that local conditions may limit our ability to construct general theories of crimes such as homicide. Yet there were some consistencies. Perhaps the most notable finding, and the one most central to the purpose of this book, is that the independent effect of immigration on homicide was negative and statistically significant, or null, in five of the six models. The immigrant/homicide relationship was significant in two instances for blacks, exerting a contradictory effect in Miami and San Diego, and negative and significant for Latinos in El Paso. In general, immigration in these three border cities does not have the positive effect that popular stereotypes and sociological theories would predict, with one possible exception.

As for the exception, an examination of homicide case files makes clear that the positive and significant effect of immigration on black homicide events in San Diego is not a function of immigrant offenders, since most of these events are black-on-black homicides, but is most likely related to disorganization issues like the neighborhood ethnic heterogeneity associated with immigration. One possible interpretation is that homicides in San Diego are more likely to involve intergroup conflicts involving new immigrants and black residents. Another is that new immigrants tend to settle in San Diego communities with preexisting high levels of black-on-black homicide. The latter possibility complements the complex relationships among race/ethnicity, immigration, and crime uncovered by research on metropolitan New York (Alba et al., 1994). It is plausible that immigrants who settle in predominantly black neighborhoods are not present in sufficient numbers to strengthen local institutions and may in fact be contributing to the disorganization of these areas. Regardless of the explanation, it is important to bear in mind that San Diego has a low homicide rate relative to cities of a similar size (i.e., over one million people, see Martinez and Lee, 2000b).

Further analysis is certainly necessary to gain a more complete understanding of the immigration finding for the black San Diego model. I should note that this result demonstrates the value of racially disaggregated studies of homicide, since models for all racial and ethnic groups combined (not reported here) showed a uniformly negative relationship between immigration and homicide. Presenting these models, instead of the group-specific ones, would have obscured the interesting relationship revealed by the San Diego black model.

It is also important not to obscure the general thrust of the results, which in these three border cities does not support either the popular stereotypes of the impact of immigration on crime or the expectations derived from sociological theories. For example, the relationship between immigration and black homicide in Miami provides especially strong support for our counterclaim, both in the statistical results presented here and a separate spatial analysis found in Chapter 5.

Another fairly consistent finding from the quantitative results is that indicators of economic deprivation, labor market involvement, and residential instability are related to Latino and black victimization in the three cities. Unlike the result for immigration, these findings are entirely in keeping with the expectations of opportunity structure and social disorganization perspectives on the conditions that give rise to crime in urban areas. The poverty rate is the most consistent of the three indicators, exhibiting a significant, positive association with homicide in five of the six models. Instability is significant in four models and joblessness is significant in three. The latter finding is in line with recent research that suggests Latinos are poor but working, while blacks are more likely to be both poor and jobless, since male joblessness was a significant predictor of homicide in all three black models but in none of the Latino models (Logan, Alba, and McNulty, 1994; Waldinger, 1996; Wilson and Martin, 1982). So, although I find some differences across these indicators for the different cities and ethnic groups, together they provide a theoretically coherent picture of the economic and social conditions associated with elevated levels of violent victimization for urban Latinos and African Americans.

The measures of age and family structures (i.e., young males and female-headed families with children) produced findings that are at odds with predictions from the literature. In no case did either of these variables have the

expected positive, statistically significant effect. The lack
of a positive association between young males and
homicide is consistent with other research (M. R. Lee,
2000). The female-headed family variable, long thought to
contribute to a host of community problems such as crime,
depression, and joblessness, among others, did not
independently increase homicide in this study – a finding
that is in line with recent research that challenges the
conventional wisdom on the "pathology of matriarchy"
(Biblarz and Raftery, 1999:322; see also Mizell, 1999). In
fact, in two cities I observed a negative relationship
between female-headed families and homicide (Latinos in
Miami and blacks in San Diego). Of course, the null
findings might simply reflect the covariation of the family
structure indicator with the poverty rate. If the primary
influence of female-headed families on homicide is through
their elevated levels of poverty, then controlling for poverty
should eliminate their effect on homicide. Regardless of
the empirical indications that single-parent families do not
inevitably produce crime or other social pathologies, there
is little basis in existing criminological theory or prior
research for anticipating a *negative* relationship between
female-headed family structures and homicide, with
poverty and other measures of economic marginalization
controlled.

Although my present focus is on immigration, the
results suggest that decomposing the relatively crude
measure of family structure employed in most studies of
homicide (including this one) offers great potential for
theoretical advancement. Researchers have devoted
substantial efforts to explicating the complex relationship
between material resources and family structure (Corcoran,
1995), and homicide research must begin to consider these
complexities. For example, there are good reasons for
economically disadvantaged women to avoid marriage,
with many believing that marriage will not contribute

additional resources to the family unit, although it may have *negative* consequences (e.g., domestic violence, see Edin 2000). In addition, classic research by Carol Stack (1974) suggests that kinship networks may mediate the potentially deleterious effects of female-headed families. By building on the insights of this work, researchers can construct more sophisticated models of the social processes and networks that influence family structure in urban areas, thus contributing to our ability to place crime in its proper social context.

Having explored the similarities and differences across models, I now turn to the special case of black homicide in El Paso, the one example where the idiosyncrasies of race and place superseded many of the expected relationships between homicide and common covariates. Recall that in this model, neither the risk variable (population) nor poverty was significantly related to black homicide. Without an understanding of the social context of the black population of this city, these results would seem counterintuitive. However, El Paso does not have the problem of concentrated black poverty to the same extent as the deindustrializing cities of the Northeast and Midwest – cities on which so much of our knowledge of homicide has been based. In fact, El Paso has a relatively small number of black residents compared to most large cities, and many of them are employed by the military and therefore have stable employment. Although poverty and the number of black residents do not exert independent effects on black homicide, neighborhoods with high levels of black male joblessness and residential "instability" (not a race-specific variable) exhibit comparatively high levels of black homicide. The differences in findings across the three cities reinforce the view that policies designed to reduce violence must consider important differences in the local context in which violence is situated.

Although the quantitative results presented in this chapter are informative, much more research is required before we will gain a definitive understanding of the link between immigration and homicide. The following specific caveats are especially warranted. First, in order to focus on immigration as a macrological process this study ignored individual-level issues regarding whether either the perpetrators or victims of homicide were immigrants. I have directed attention to the conditions of communities that are associated with variation in group levels of criminal violence and made no claims about the individual-level relationships among violence, poverty, immigrant-status, and other factors within communities. Although this approach avoids the ecological fallacy (i.e., the attribution to the individual level of group-level relationships), future work should integrate both individual and community levels of analysis to the extent that data availability will allow. Furthermore, the circumstances under which people immigrate (e.g., political or economic), as well as the segmented assimilation of specific immigrant groups into the core and peripheral economies of urban areas (Logan et al., 2000), likely have important implications for urban crime. The recent immigration of diverse groups of people into large American cities has significantly complicated the relationship between race/ethnicity and violent crime. Yet most studies continue to gloss over this complexity, often dropping high-immigration cities like Miami from their analyses (Parker and McCall 1999). While it was useful to examine the effect of "immigration" on crime, given our current lack of knowledge, future work must attempt to model the effects of specific groups of immigrants, or different segments within a particular immigrant group (e.g., professionals versus laborers), in order to more fully understand the immigration/crime nexus.

Second, distinguishing legal from illegal immigrants might be a potentially useful strategy in crime research and immigration policies (e.g., deportation) that could prevent future violence in many communities. There is however little evidence that "illegal" immigrants are over involved in violent crime, or at least much more so than "legal" immigrants (Hagan and Palloni, 1998), even though it is clear that most immigrants live on the economic margins of society. Also, "illegal aliens" cannot be thoroughly separated from legal ones at the local level. It is difficult to single out a community where illegal aliens outnumber legal immigrants, or even a series of street blocks where "illegals" are distinguishable from others. Instead, many are blended into poor Latino families and neighborhoods. Forcibly separating them from their communities through deportation tends to break up families and weaken social bonds and community cohesion, thereby disrupting local conditions. This policy "solution" thereby wreaks more havoc on disadvantaged communities, adding to the consequences of adverse structural conditions. Rather than encouraging a clandestine life, steps to integrate those without "papers" into legal residents would probably prove less harmful in the long run than the traditional use of deportation.

A third concern relates to the cross-sectional nature of the data on which the quantitative analysis was based. A longitudinal analysis is required to advance our understanding of the causal ordering among variables such as immigration, residential instability, poverty, and the ethnic composition of neighborhoods. For example, it is possible that immigration into a given neighborhood may contribute to an increase in residential instability at a later time, which might then shape subsequent homicide levels in that neighborhood or surrounding areas. Future research should therefore employ a longitudinal design in order to disentangle the causal ordering of neighborhood-level social processes that unfold over a period of years and that influence patterns of violent crime.

Conclusion

Notwithstanding these concerns, the major finding of this chapter – that recent immigration generally does not increase community levels of homicide – has implications for policies that target immigration as a social problem. The results presented here offer little support for claims that immigration fosters homicide in three large and ethnically diverse border cities.   Indeed, native and immigrant groups alike could profit greatly from research into the counterclaim that immigration can be a stabilizing force that suppresses criminal violence. Sociologists have argued that explanations of urban crime require a "somewhat complex story line" (Alba et al. 1994:417). The data presented in this chapter suggest that the transformation of large U.S. cities by the latest wave of immigration has added a theoretically unexpected plot twist that, if replicated, will substantially alter the way this story is told.

CHAPTER 5

Geographic Patterns and Time Trends

This chapter compliments the cross-sectional, multivariate analysis in Chapter 4 by examining spatial and temporal issues surrounding ethnicity, immigration, and homicide in the three border cities. In the first part, I use maps of homicides and selected structural characteristics to provide a more detailed picture of the spatial distribution of homicide. These maps reveal patterns that are not captured in the statistical models. In the second part, I present graphs of homicide trends over time, with special attention to ethnicity and immigration. As with the maps, these graphs address questions about homicide in the three cities that were not explored in the previous chapter. The analyses in this chapter also raise questions that should guide future research, both quantitative and qualitative.

Spatial Analysis

Spatial analysis has a long history in social science, particularly in the sociology of crime. For example, scholars associated with the Chicago school of sociology (e.g., Shaw and McKay, 1931) used maps of crime events to make theoretical points about the relationship of social disorganization and crime. With the advent of powerful personal computers, crime mapping (see Weisburd and McEwen, 1997), as well as statistical spatial analytic techniques (see Anselin et al., 2000), have recently assumed a prominent place in sociological studies.

In Chapter 3, I outlined the research strategies that guide this study, including the presentation of maps that follow. Recall my discussion of the pioneering work of Shaw and McKay (1931; 1969) and others (e.g., Lind, 1930a; 1930b) who used maps to explore crime patterns in specific areas of cities. These scholars provided powerful evidence that crime could not be "explained" by theories that were derived from studies of large, undifferentiated aggregations (i.e., cities, states, nations, etc.). For example, poverty is often linked to high levels of crime and as a result has been widely used as an explanatory variable. Yet Lind (1930a; 1930b) pointed out that an examination of two neighborhoods with similar poverty characteristics had widely differing rates of crime. Both neighborhoods also had high levels of immigrants, but the low-crime area turned out to be ethnically homogeneous, while the high-crime one contained a variety of ethnic groups.

This suggests that presenting only the city-wide statistical results in Chapter 4 would advance a partial understanding of ethnicity, immigration, and homicide. Therefore, in the following section I use maps to explore intra-city variations that might be obscured in the statistical models. This presentation is not exhaustive, but rather illustrative of the value of spatial analysis, since I only explore one issue in each city.

Furthermore, the selection of areas in each city is purposive, not random, since the populations of interest (e.g., Haitians, Asians) tend to be concentrated in certain sections of the cities. Additional guidelines for the selection of tracts included dropping tracts with comparatively small numbers of residents, little variation in variables of interest, or insufficient numbers of homicide events (which would render homicide rates meaningless).[21] Despite this selection "bias," the maps remain useful because they address questions that cannot be answered with the Poisson models. Future research could explore other areas to determine whether the results vary by group or location.

Black Homicide and Haitian Immigration in Miami

The first set of maps explores the immigration/homicide relationship in predominantly African American and Haitian census tracts in the northern part of Miami. In this map, I am interested in whether the city-wide relationship between recent immigration and black homicide holds for this subset of Miami census tracts (recall from Table 4.6 that this relationship was negative and significant). I have selected five predominantly African American tracts in the Liberty City section of Miami for comparison with seven adjacent tracts in the Little Haiti section – as the name implies, an area with a large proportion of recent arrivals from Haiti. Both locations are overwhelmingly black (on average, the population of the twelve tracts is 88.7% black).

A focus on these two Miami neighborhoods allows us to test the notion that compositional heterogeneity disrupts a community's regulatory capacity, which has been elaborated and widely disseminated by contemporary social disorganization scholars (cf. Bursik 1999). Warner (1999) has concisely summarized current thinking: "Heterogeneity also diminishes community ties, as racial and ethnic differences among people may impose barriers to friendships and broad-based organizational ties, thereby limiting the breadth of neighborhood networks and the consequential potential for informal control" (p. 101). Crime rates are likely to be much higher under these conditions.

On the other hand, recent research on African-American ghettos has indicated that homogeneous areas are not better organized for social control (Anderson, 1990);

rather, residents in these areas suffer from the concentration of multiple social problems (Wilson, 1987; Sampson and Wilson, 1995). Furthermore, the economic experiences of some groups of recent immigrants in ethnic enclaves differ markedly from those of earlier generations, suggesting that established ideas about immigration require updating (Portes and Stepick, 1993; Portes and Rumbaut, 2001). Ethnically heterogeneous immigrant communities, while often quite poor, have contributed to a revitalization of familial, social, and economic institutions that offers their residents significant advantages.

Thus, existing research suggests two contradictory views of "ghettos" and "slums." Proponents of the *social disorganization perspective* have argued that crime should flourish in heterogeneous slums in which immigrants settle. However, advocates of the *concentrated disadvantage perspective* might respond that levels of crime should be higher in homogeneous ghetto areas that suffer from long-standing economic deprivation. Scholars associated with the recently emerging *immigration revitalization perspective* tend to support the latter perspective by through research showing that ghetto residents have not benefited from the "enclave economies" that have revitalized some immigrant slums (cf. Portes and Rumbaut, 2001). The predictions and explanations of these perspectives with respect to the two northern Miami neighborhoods are summarized in Table 5.1.

As Figure 5.1 shows, moving from left to right across the map (i.e., west to east), the black homicide rate systematically decreases as the presence of immigrants (largely Haitian) increases. Black homicide rates are

Table 5.1: Predictions about Immigration, Ethnic Heterogeneity, and Crime

Perspective	Prediction	Explanation
Social Disorganization	Heterogeneous slums will exhibit higher levels of crime than homogeneous ghettos. Therefore, homicide levels will be higher in Little Haiti.	Immigration increases *residential instability* and *ethnic heterogeneity*, which weakens social control, thereby increasing crime.
Concentrated Disadvantage	Homogeneous ghettos will exhibit higher levels of crime than heterogeneous slums. Therefore, homicide levels will be higher in Liberty City.	*Concentrated disadvantage* associated with *ethnic homogeneity* weakens social control, thereby increasing crime.
Immigration Revitalization	Homogeneous ghettos will exhibit higher levels of crime than heterogeneous slums. Therefore, homicide levels will be lower in Little Haiti.	Immigration revitalizes poor areas and strengthens social control (thereby decreasing crime) due to *strong familial and neighborhood institutions* and enhanced job opportunities associated with *enclave economies.*

Source: The predictions and explanations of the social disorganization perspective were derived from the classic work of Shaw and McKay (1931) and Lind (1930a; 1930b); concentrated disadvantage draws on Wilson (1987) and Sampson and Wilson (1995); immigration revitalization is based on Portes and Stepick (1993), Portes and Rumbaut (2001), and Lee et al. (2001).

highest in the northwest part of Liberty City (tract 1903 = an annualized rate of 159.24 per 100,000; tract 1501 = 149.03) and lowest in the southeast corner of Little Haiti (tract 2201 = 23.22; tract 2004 = 26.53). Conversely, recent immigration is highest in eastern tracts of Little Haiti (tract 1402 = 42 percent; tract 2004 = 38 percent) and lowest in northwestern Liberty City (tract 1501 = 0.82 percent; tract 1901 = 4.5 percent).

The percentage of black poverty varies, with the highest poverty tracts located in both Liberty City and immigrant-heavy Little Haiti. The highest homicide tracts (1903 and 1501) also exhibit high levels of poverty (58 percent and 68 percent, respectively). But comparatively low homicide rate tracts in Little Haiti have similarly high levels of poverty (e.g., tract 2004 = 57 percent; tract 2003 = 50 percent). As Figure 5.1 demonstrates, the relationship between homicide and poverty is by no means linear in the two neighborhoods. Furthermore, tract 1904 in Liberty City has a relatively high level of homicide, but low levels both of recent immigration and poverty. It appears from a tract-by-tract comparison of the three figures that poverty is positively related to black homicide in some tracts in northern Miami but that this association is not as strong as the inverse relationship between immigration and black homicide.

Figures 5.2-5.4 display the relationship in a more visual manner, using shading instead of numbers. Regardless of the method used to display the data, Haitian immigration seems to be more closely linked with homicide in this area of Miami than poverty, and the presence of immigrants does not appear to have the disorganizing effect predicted by theory, at least as measured by tract levels of black homicide. The maps verify that the negative effect of the immigration variable (which included all immigrants, not just Haitians) in the Miami black regression model, holds for the predominantly African American and Haitian

Figure 5.1: Black Homicide (1985-1995), Black Poverty (1990), and Recent Immigration (1980-1990) in Northern Miami

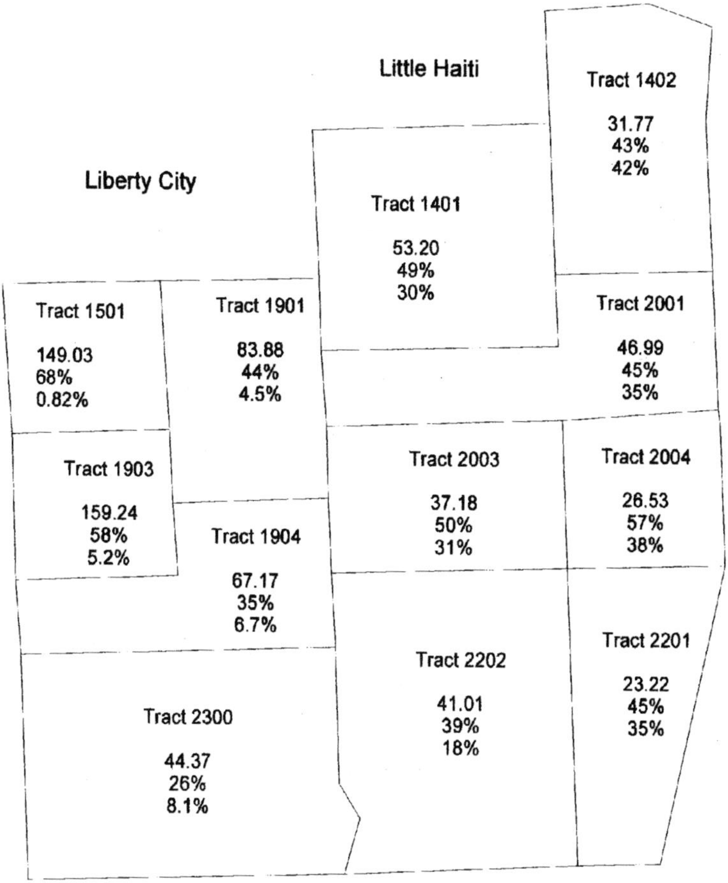

Little Haiti

Tract 1402

31.77
43%
42%

Liberty City

Tract 1401

53.20
49%
30%

Tract 1501

149.03
68%
0.82%

Tract 1901

83.88
44%
4.5%

Tract 2001

46.99
45%
35%

Tract 1903

159.24
58%
5.2%

Tract 1904

67.17
35%
6.7%

Tract 2003

37.18
50%
31%

Tract 2004

26.53
57%
38%

Tract 2201

23.22
45%
35%

Tract 2202

41.01
39%
18%

Tract 2300

44.37
26%
8.1%

Numbers in each tract appear as follows:
Black Homicide Rate
Percent Black Poverty
Percent New Immigrant

Figure 5.2: Black Homicide Rates in Northern Miami, 1985-1995

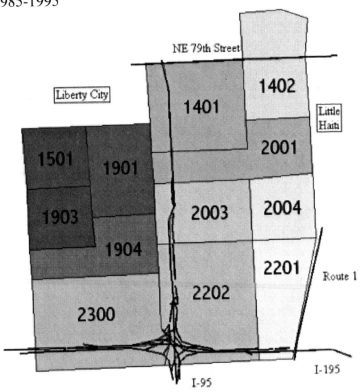

Note: Darker shading indicates higher black homicide rates.

Figure 5.3: Recent Immigration in Northern Miami, 1980-1990

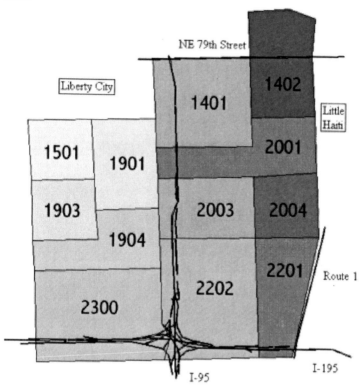

Note: Darker shading indicates higher levels of recent immigration.

Figure 5.4: Black Poverty in Northern Miami, 1990

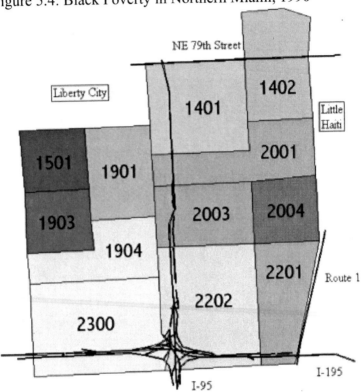

Note: Darker shading indicates higher black poverty.

section of the city (where the recent immigrants are largely Haitian).

Of course the maps do not statistically control for other structural covariates of homicide, and indeed this is not possible given the small number of tracts, but it does provide a visual sense of the spatial distribution of immigration and homicide that cannot be accounted for by tract levels of one prominent predictor (i.e., poverty). In fact, the other variables used in the statistical model presented in Chapter 4 do not show the same degree of systematic variation with homicide in this part of the city as the immigration variable does, which suggests that the magnitude of the negative immigration/homicide relationship is even stronger in these twelve tracts when compared with the moderate relationship found in the city-wide Poisson regression model.

Figure 5.5 shows the locations of all of the African American and Haitian homicides in northern Miami. This "spot map" technique is useful for identifying intra-tract locations with a high level of homicide (i.e., "hot spots). Note that multiple homicides occurred at roughly the same location over the years, which means that the symbols on the map are stacked and thus not all are visible. This may give the impression that there are fewer homicides in a given tract. This stacking is an issue mainly for Liberty City tracts 1501, 1903, and 1904, but even with this problem the spot map still conveys the fact that homicide levels are high in these tracts.

While some overlap between African American and Haitian homicide is apparent, it is also clear that African American homicides are densely concentrated in the northwest corner of Liberty City, while Haitians are killed almost exclusively in the Little Haiti section of this area. Thus, homicide victimization strongly reflects settlement patterns, and African American homicide is especially

Figure 5.5: African American and Haitian Homicide
Victims in Northern Miami, 1985-1995

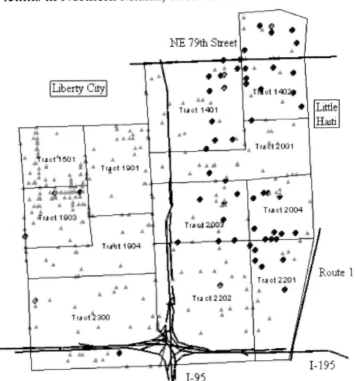

Note: Triangles indicate African American homicide
victims, dots indicate Haitian homicide victims.

prevalent in a handful of tracts (i.e., hot spots) where few or
no Haitians are killed (e.g., tracts 1501 and 1903).

This section demonstrated the utility of maps for
overcoming limitations of statistical methods when
studying populations of recent immigrant groups (e.g.,
Haitians) concentrated in a single area of a city. This case
study provided a test of the predictions of three theoretical
perspectives regarding immigration, ethnicity, and crime
(see Table 5.1). The social disorganization model predicts
that ethnically heterogeneous immigrant "slums" should

exhibit higher rates of crime than similarly impoverished but homogeneous "ghettos"; the concentrated disadvantage and immigration revitalization perspectives predict the opposite.

At least in terms of the violent crime of homicide, the maps did not support the disorganization thesis. Black homicide was inversely related to immigration. Haitians had much lower rates of homicide involvement than similarly located African Americans, despite comparable levels of poverty in specific tracts and the fact that Haitians in south Florida "encounter even more prejudice than other blacks" (Stepick, 1998:115). If immigration and associated ethnic heterogeneity were positively related to homicide levels in contemporary society, we would expect to see this relationship most strongly in these 12 census tracts from northern Miami. We do not, a result that suggests that the social disorganization perspective on crime may be overdue for reformulation. The maps support a concentrated disadvantage view of Liberty City, while providing initial evidence that Haitians have revitalized, rather than disorganized, the area of northern Miami in which they have settled. Factors contributing to the high rates of homicide in black ghettos such as Liberty City are well-known (Sampson and Wilson, 1995; Wilson, 1987). Less understood are the ways in which immigration may revitalize an area and thereby suppress violent crime, an issue I explore in Chapter 6.

Latino Homicide and Immigration in El Paso

Turning to El Paso, I now investigate whether a similar relationship between immigration and homicide exists for predominantly Latino areas. In the Poisson model for this city, the new immigrant variable was negatively related to homicide, and this relationship was statistically significant. The issue here is whether this relationship remains negative based on a map of a selected area with comparatively high proportions of immigrants, in this case Mexicans.

Figure 5.6 is set up similar to Figure 5.1 and shows ten tracts from southeast El Paso that vary dramatically in terms of both homicide rates and immigrants (as a point of reference, tracts 3802 and 3903 are bounded by the Rio Grande). Some are in the highest quartile of all tracts in El Paso in terms of homicide (tracts 3902 and 3903) and immigrants (3902 and 4103); some are in the lowest quartile (3901, 4103) and (4107), respectively. The rest of the tracts fall within the middle two quartiles.

Unlike the obvious inverse immigration/homicide relationship in the black area of northern Miami shown in Figures 5.1-5.4, the immigration/homicide pattern for Latinos in this part of El Paso is not clear at first glance. Shaded maps are of little value here and are not provided for this area. The lack of a clear relationship in southeast El Paso highlights the importance of examining the spatial patterns of racially/ethnically disaggregated violent crime data. Although there is no overarching directional trend, homicide rates are lowest in tracts *not* located in the northern or southern extremes (3901, 3802, 4103). Further, high homicide rates are associated with high levels of immigrants in some tracts (3902, 3903) but not others (4107, 4103, 3901).

For example, no homicides occurred in tract 3901 (the Ysleta area) during the 1985-1994 time period, despite the fact that this tract had a high level of new immigrants (8.3%) and Latino poverty (41%) relative to other tracts in the city. On the other hand, one of the highest percentages of new immigrants in this part of El Paso is found in tract 3902 (12% of residents in this tract immigrated during the 1980-1990 time period) and this tract also had the highest Latino homicide rate (15.6) in the southeast part of the city. This shows that blanket statements about the immigration/homicide connection that may be valid for the

Figure 5.6: Latino Homicide (1985-1995), Latino Poverty (1990), and Recent Immigration (1980-1990) in Southeast El Paso

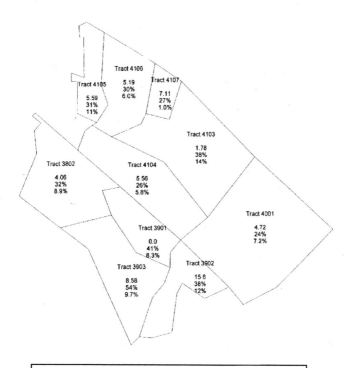

Numbers in each tract appear as follows:
Latino Homicide Rate
Percent Latino Poverty
Percent New Immigrant

city as a whole do not apply to smaller aggregations like individual census tracts. This is an important point, because residents may care little for city-wide trends when their local situation is much different.

To provide some additional context, I note that Latino homicide rates and the percent of new immigrants were essentially uncorrelated in these ten tracts (r=.08). Latino Poverty, also shown in Figure 5.6, was also generally unrelated to Latino homicide in this part of the city (r=.15). Of course, this does not refute the strong city-wide finding for Latino poverty as a predictor of homicide in the Poisson model, because these tracts range from poor (24% below the poverty line) to very poor (54%). However, in this economically depressed area other factors besides immigration or poverty may be shaping tract levels of homicide.

Since the relationship between immigration and Latino homicide in this section of El Paso was not as straightforward as the one between immigration and black homicide in north Miami (as presented in Figure 5.1), I decided to further explore the El Paso area using another mapping method. After debating a number of possibilities, I concluded that it would be useful to show the spatial distribution of homicide by plotting individual homicide events, rather than displaying aggregated rates.

Since research has found that distinct types of homicide are influenced by different structural characteristics (cf. Avakame, 1998; Martinez, 2000), I opted to examine the homicides about which public fear is the greatest (e.g., involving gangs or strangers) rather than others types (e.g., domestic). It is reasonable to assume that public opinion on immigration might be more negative if immigrants tend to reside in areas associated with gang or stranger violence, because people may link immigration to "unsafe" streets.

I test whether this kind of homicide tends to occur in areas with higher levels of immigrants by plotting what I call "public anxiety homicides" involving victims of all ethnicities for the same section of the city that appears in Figure 5.6. These homicides include gang-related, stranger, and cases where the motive was unknown and no victim/offender relationship was identified. These types are of special public concern because they usually occur in public spaces, as opposed to the more "private" disputes among intimates, and often appear "random" in the sense that any resident of this predominantly Latino area might be a target.

The public anxiety homicides shown in Figure 5.7 generally occur in the outlying parts of this section of El Paso; the area in the middle of the map has none. Note that only thirteen such homicides occurred for this entire area over the ten-year period for which data were available. The tracts in this Figure also show the percent of recent immigrants, but the relationship of this demographic characteristic with the killings is not uniform and is complicated by the fact that many homicides occur on the border of two tracts. Based on this evidence, then, the proportion of recent immigrants at the tract level in this part of El Paso does not seem systematically linked to the kinds of homicides that generate the most public fear, and indeed, there were only a handful of these cases in this part of El Paso. Again, this analysis should be expanded to cover other areas of the city, but given current space constraints this discussion merely serves to illustrate the value of plotting homicides as a means to further investigate tract-level trends.

Black Homicide and Immigration in San Diego

The immigration/homicide link was fairly clear in the Miami map but more complex in the El Paso maps. The situation is even more complicated in the area of southeast San Diego displayed in Figure 5.8, due in part to that area's

Figure 5.7: "Public Anxiety" Homicides (1985-1995) and
Recent Immigration (1980-1990) in Southeast El Paso

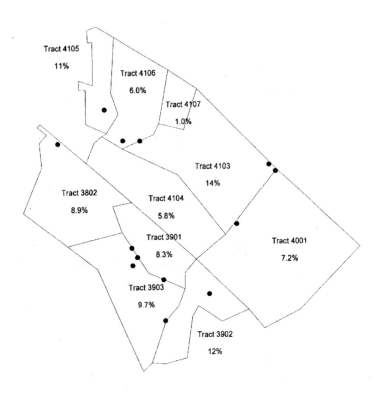

Dots indicate the location of
"public anxiety" homicides

Percentages refer to recent immigration

Figure 5.8: Black Homicide (1985-1995) and Recent Immigration (1980-1990) in Southeast San Diego

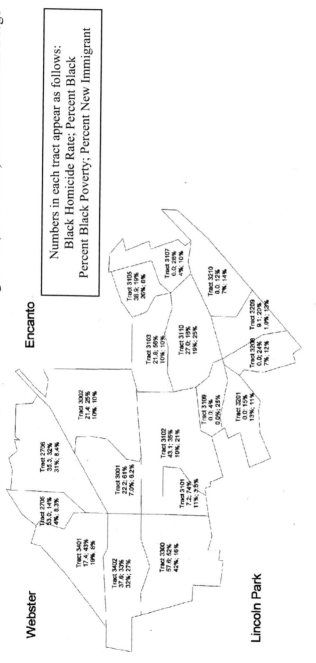

Encanto

Numbers in each tract appear as follows:
Black Homicide Rate; Percent Black
Percent Black Poverty; Percent New Immigrant

Tract 3105
36.9; 19%
26%; 6%

Tract 3107
0.0; 28%
4%; 10%

Tract 3210
0.0; 12%
7%; 14%

Tract 3103
21.8; 56%
10%; 10%

Tract 3110
27.0; 16%
19%; 25%

Tract 3209
9.1; 20%
1.0%; 13%

Tract 3208
0.0; 24%
7%; 12%

Tract 3002
21.4; 25%
10%; 10%

Tract 2706
35.3; 32%
31%; 8.4%

Tract 2705
53.0; 14%
4%; 8.3%

Tract 3001
22.2; 61%
7.0%; 6.2%

Tract 3102
43.1; 35%
10%; 21%

Tract 3109
0.0; 4%
0.0%; 25%

Tract 3201
0.0; 15%
13%; 11%

Tract 3101
7.2; 74%
11%; 3.5%

Tract 3401
17.4; 43%
19%; 8%

Tract 3402
37.6; 33%
32%; 27%

Tract 3300
57.6; 52%
42%; 16%

Webster

Lincoln Park

Paradise Hills

ethnic heterogeneity. Still, the mapping strategies utilized in the previous sections can be used to illuminate some of the factors underlying this complexity.

Remember from Table 4.6 that the Poisson model for black homicides in San Diego was the only model where the relationship between the immigration variable and the dependent variable was positive and significant. Because black homicides in San Diego overwhelmingly involved black victims and offenders I conjectured that immigration as a social process might be disrupting black communities and contributing to higher levels of black-on-black homicide (as opposed to the explanation that an influx of immigrant offenders were responsible for the positive and significant coefficient). In this section I investigate this notion in an ethnically mixed part of San Diego that also contains a large black population.

Ethnic heterogeneity has long been an important consideration in the social disorganization framework (Lind, 1930a; 1930b; Shaw and McKay, 1931), and since the eighteen tracts shown in Figure 5.8 are ethnically diverse I have added the percentage of black residents in each tract to the three community features displayed in the previous maps. After all, when Lind (1930b) compared two adjacent neighborhoods he found that economically disadvantaged areas with homogeneous populations had lower levels of crime than ethnically mixed areas with similar structural characteristics. Unfortunately, the situation described by Lind in the 1930s is not analogous to this part of San Diego in the 1980s and 1990s, since immigration and within-city migration has rendered practically all of the tracts in this area ethnically diverse. At best, a few of the tracts have simple black majorities. The important issue is whether immigrants in this part of San Diego are associated with greater heterogeneity (as measured by a comparatively low percentage of black residents), which in turn is associated with high black homicide rates.

Figure 5.8 does not allow for a simple resolution to this issue because there is no clear-cut trend. For example, a comparison of tract 3300 with tract 3101 (Lincoln Park area) appears to support the hypothesis stated above [but note that the black poverty level in tract 3300 is four times greater than that in tract 3101]. However, a focus on two tracts is misleading since numerous counter-examples can also be found. Tracts in the Paradise Hills area (3109, 3201, 3208, 3209, 3210) contain a substantial proportion of immigrants, a low proportion of blacks, and virtually no black homicide. Low black poverty is also a feature of these tracts, again suggesting that ethnic heterogeneity and immigration are less crucial than basic economic conditions.[22]

Bivariate correlations for these tracts can help clear up some of the visual confusion in apparent Figure 5.8. Black poverty in these tracts is highly correlated with the black homicide rate (r=.55), but homicide is not correlated with the percentage of black residents (r=.07) or the percentage of new immigrants (r=.05). Taken as a whole, poverty seems most important in shaping black homicide in southeastern San Diego, but again, a tract-by-tract examination points out that there are exceptions (e.g., tract 2705).

Ideally, Figure 5.8 would show an unambiguous pattern that would compliment the Poisson results presented in Table 4.6 in a straightforward manner. However, at this point the spatial distribution is complex and does not permit parsimonious conclusions. Therefore, I have again followed an alternative mapping strategy by plotting individual black homicide events in order to better understand the spatial trends. Figure 5.9 shows all of the black homicide victims in the eighteen tracts I have selected. Referring to Figures 5.8 and 5.9, it does seem that

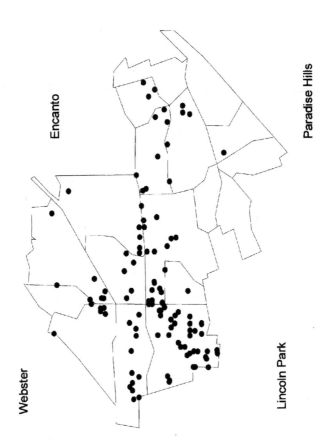

Figure 5.9: Black Homicides in Southeast San Diego, 1985-1995

Figure 5.10: Black Gang-Related Homicides in Southeast San Diego, 1985-1995

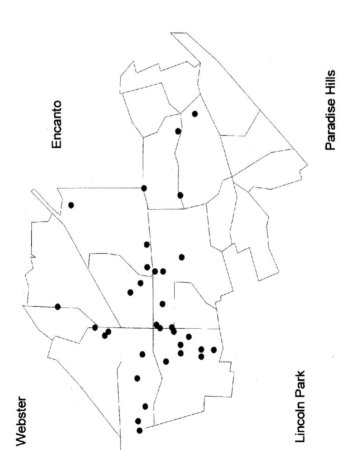

Figure 5.11: Asian Gang-Related Homicides in Southeast San Diego, 1985-1995

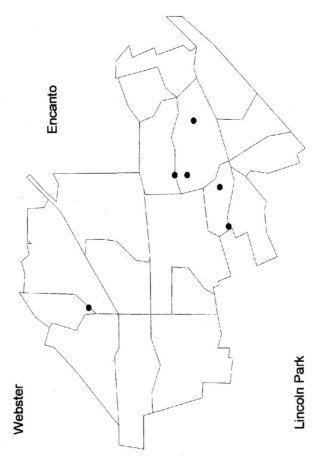

black homicides tend to be concentrated in tracts with relatively high proportions of immigrants (i.e., tracts 3300, 3402, and 3102), but these tracts also have comparatively high proportions of black poverty.

One way to shed further light on the black homicide situation is to examine the location of known gang-related homicides. It is certainly possible that gang activity is playing a key role in the distribution of black homicide in this part of the city. Figure 5.10 shows all of the black victims of gang-related violence in this part of San Diego. This distribution largely conforms to the total black homicide pattern from Figure 5.9, indicating that a connection exists. It is also possible that the gang activities of immigrant groups might shape the distribution of black homicides, but the Asian victims of gang homicides in Figure 5.11 (what few there are) tend to occur in the Paradise Hills area, while black victims of gangs (and black victims generally) tend to cluster in the Lincoln Park area. The evidence provided by this snapshot of the spatial distribution of gang homicide in southeastern San Diego does not suggest that the distribution of Asian gang homicides is closely related to patterns of black homicide in the way that black gang homicides are.

Temporal Analysis

In addition to these spatial issues, an examination of trends over time can reveal additional features about the nature of homicide in the three cities. Recall that Table 4.1 in the previous chapter provided a broad picture of homicide levels by ethnicity; Figures 5.12, 5.13, and 5.14 in the current chapter offer more detail about the change over time in these levels, and how these changes track with the numbers of immigrants to each city. Because the new immigrant variable was constructed using census counts of immigrants who arrived in the United States during the

1980-1990 time period, and the dependent variable aggregates homicides from 1985-1995, to provide more context group-specific homicide rates are shown from 1980-1995. In these Figures, homicide rates are expressed per 100,000 group-specific residents, and immigration counts are expressed in hundreds, so that both the rates and counts could be graphed on the same Figure.[23] One caveat is warranted: while immigrant counts *might* be expected to track the homicide rates of groups residing in areas where immigrants tend to settle (i.e., Latinos, Haitians, Asians), if immigrants are in fact crime-prone, any relationship between immigrant counts and the rates of other groups who have less contact with immigrants (i.e., blacks and Anglos) are more likely to be spurious.

Homicide and Immigration in El Paso

Figure 5.12 displays city-wide homicide and immigration trends for El Paso from 1980-1994 (recall that 1995 homicide data were not available for this city). It appears that the immigration trend, which started high in 1980 (around 5,000 per year), dropped to a low in 1983, then rose and leveled off in 1987, does not track with homicide rates. The Anglo and Latino rates remained consistently low throughout the 15 year period, but the black rate rose sharply after 1988 to a high of over 30 per 100,000 in 1994.

The El Paso trends raise two points. First, changes in immigration levels do not seem to result in corresponding changes in homicide levels for any of the groups, at least during this time period. Second, the Poisson models will not be able to uncover the reason for the sharp rise in black homicide rates in the 1990s, since the census data are only available for one time point (i.e., 1990). While the Poisson models are valuable for other reasons, clearly the upward trend in black homicide rates ought to be explored in future research.

Figure 5.12: El Paso Homicide Rates and Count of Recent Immigrants

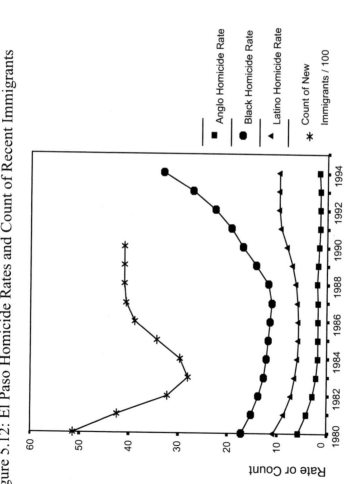

Homicide and Immigration in Miami

A different picture emerges for Miami, as shown in Figure 5.13. Here black homicide rates do seem to track the immigration counts, a finding that casts the immigration/black homicide relationship in a potentially different light compared to the Poisson results and the map of north Miami discussed earlier. But available research and theory cannot account for this finding, and changes in the black homicide rate may be the result of some other unmeasured variable (e.g., the rise of systemic violence associated with the crack cocaine market). Interestingly, the Haitian homicide rate remained the lowest of all groups during this 16 year period, and did not track with the immigration counts. The Anglo and Latino rates also did not vary in a similar manner as the immigration trend, with the exception that all three declined sharply in the early 1980s. By the late 1980s, the Anglo, Haitian, and Latino rates converged at a low level, at least as compared with the black homicide rate in Miami. Again, it is difficult to disentangle the reasons for a rise or decline in any of the homicide trends using Poisson regression, but so far the Figures make it clear that aggregating all of these groups together would obscure important differences.

Homicide and Immigration in San Diego

The immigration pattern in San Diego shown in Figure 5.14 is quite similar to the other cities: it begins with a peak in 1980 (in this case just below 14,000), declines to a low in 1983, and rises and levels off in the late 1980s around 10,000. While the Asian homicide rate might be expected to track the immigration count somewhat, it remains relatively flat and is the lowest of all groups throughout the 1980s. It does rise slightly in the 1990s. The Anglo, black, and Latino rates also increase in the 1990s, though the

Figure 5.13: Miami Homicide Rates and Count of Recent Immigrants

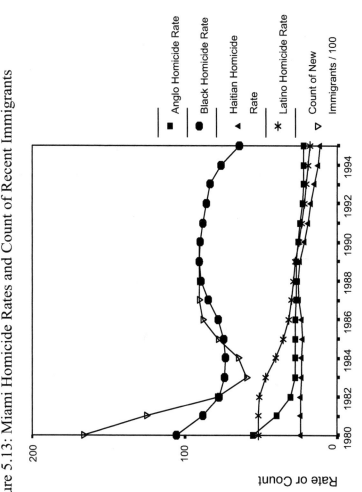

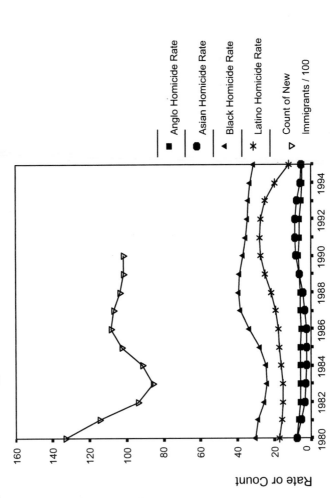

Figure 5.14: San Diego Homicide Rates and Count of Recent Immigrants

Latino rate begins a sharp decline by 1993. As with the other cities, it is difficult to say precisely why the rates behave as they do, and again the Poisson models cannot address this issue.

These Figures can be used to draw three important conclusions. First, Table 4.1 from the previous chapter demonstrated that homicide varies widely by race and place; the Figures provide support for this finding and show that homicide also varies over time, sometimes considerably (e.g., blacks in El Paso). Second, immigration levels do not seem to inflate the homicide rates of the groups that it should impact the strongest (e.g., Latinos, Asians, and Haitians). And third, rates for specific immigrant groups (i.e., Asians and Haitians) were often the lowest in their respective city, casting doubt on the commonly assumed link between immigrants and crime.

Conclusion

This chapter assessed the complex connections between ethnicity, immigration, and homicide in a manner that considered the spatial and temporal context of these relationships. Thus, the purpose of this chapter was to move beyond the cross-sectional Poisson models in Chapter 4. The findings of the current chapter both support and challenge the conclusions drawn from the statistical analyses.

The homicide maps of selected areas in each city demonstrated that the relationship between immigration and homicide can be quite simple, as in north Miami, or complex, as in El Paso and especially San Diego. The Poisson models were not able to convey the diversity found in the maps. Yet, the maps did seem to support the statistical models' findings regarding the relationship between tract levels of recent immigrants and group-specific levels of homicide. In this sense, the maps (and time trends) provide a means of triangulating the Poisson results.

The positive relationship between immigration and black homicide in the San Diego statistical model was found to be rather complicated, at least in the section of the city presented in the San Diego maps. A few tracts had high immigration proportions and black homicide rates, but many did not. Furthermore, the spatial distribution of Asian and black gang homicide was not similar.

Turning to the time trends, homicide rates did not generally track immigration levels in the Figures, thus complimenting the findings for the immigration variable in the Poisson models discussed in Chapter 4. Another fact revealed by the time trends (and echoed in the map shown in Figure 5.1) is the striking contrast in homicide rates between Miami's native-born blacks and immigrant Haitians. By all indications, Haitians in Miami are among the most disadvantaged groups in the country (see Portes and Stepick, 1985), yet they had the lowest homicide involvement out of all of Miami's groups over the 16 year time period for which data were available. Equally remarkable are the extremely high (though falling) rates of homicide of Miami's native-born blacks – clearly a pressing public health concern for this group, and one requires more detailed study. The exceptionally low Asian rate in San Diego is just one example which suggests that native groups could profit from a better understanding of the ways that immigrants' social capital works to suppress homicide victimization.

CHAPTER 6
Conclusion:
Immigration and the Revitalization
of Urban Communities

The statistical, spatial, and temporal analyses presented in this book were primarily concerned with advancing our understanding of ethnicity, immigration, and homicide. While the results answered many questions, at times they also seemed to suggest that this relationship is quite complex, varying over time and across locations. For example, the relatively straightforward Poisson regression results must be interpreted in light of the spatial and temporal analyses. Thus, any attempt to succinctly convey the major conclusions of this research must immediately be followed by caveats about the variations that confound simplistic explanations. Since results did vary somewhat by ethnicity, as we would expect given the literature (Parker and McCall, 1999; Ousey, 1999), I discuss the Latino and black findings separately.

Immigration and Latino Homicide

The influence of immigration on homicide should be most strongly apparent in Latino communities since most of the recent immigrants to the three cities are from Mexico or other Latin American countries. The statistical analyses revealed that immigration was not significantly related to Latino homicide in Miami and San Diego, while the relationship was negative and significant in El Paso. Furthermore, the graphs showed that changes over time in Latino homicide rates did not track changes in immigration counts. Finally, the maps of one southeast section of El Paso did not demonstrate a consistent connection between the percent of new immigrants and the spatial distribution of either Latino homicide rates or "public anxiety" homicides.

Since immigration appears not to be a key factor driving Latino homicide events in the cities under investigation, it is useful to review the factors that were most important. The Poisson models speak most directly to this issue. Recall that the population measure was strictly a control for homicide risk, since event counts were used, and that this variable was a strong, positive predictor in all three models. The other variables that exhibited strong, positive relationships with Latino homicide in all models were Latino poverty and the spatial lag. The instability index was a positive and significant predictor in El Paso and San Diego. These results suggest that immigration has been a red herring in discussions of community factors that cause violence (cf. Lamm and Imhoff, 1985; Tanton and Lutton, 1993). The findings presented in this book counsel against using immigrants as an excuse to ignore systemic issues associated with violence such as economic deprivation and instability.

The lack of a positive relationship between immigration and Latino homicide in the regression models is especially interesting given the relationship of immigrants to Latino poverty in the three cities. Correlations discussed in Lee (2000) implied that the most recent wave of immigrants tended to settle in impoverished Latino areas in El Paso and San Diego, but not in Miami. One possible interpretation is that recent immigrants of Latino origin (i.e., Cubans) in Miami have economically benefited from ties to co-ethnics who have established businesses – but this is an open question at best (Portes and Stepick, 1985). Looking at the Miami correlations, Latino joblessness appears more strongly related to Latino homicide than poverty, and joblessness is negatively related to the immigration variable. But recall also that Latino homicide rates were higher in Miami than in the other two cities, further complicating the picture.

In sum, recent immigration, male joblessness, female-headed families, and the proportion of young males did not emerge from this research as positive predictors of Latino homicide. Instead, a rather parsimonious explanation emerged from this study: Latino homicide in the three cities is a function of Latino poverty and processes external to a given census tract (as measured by the spatial lag variable), and to a lesser extent residential instability.

Immigration and Black Homicide

The link between immigration and black homicide was more equivocal than for Latino homicide. In the regression models for black homicide, the new immigrant coefficient was negative and non-significant in El Paso, negative and significant in Miami, and positive and significant in San Diego. Thus, the effect of immigration, independent of other structural influences, depends on the city in question. This was also true for the specific sections of Miami and San Diego explored in the maps: the negative relationship was demonstrated clearly in northern Miami, while the positive relationship was much more ambiguous in southeastern San Diego. In terms of time trends, black homicide rates did seem to track immigration counts in all three cities more closely than did Latino homicide rates. At this point, any explanation for this association would be pure speculation. But this issue is discussed below along with the other suggestions for future research.

As with the Latino models, it is useful to note the best predictors of black homicide across cities. Again, the population control was a strong predictor, but the only other variable that was significant in all three cities was male joblessness. Recall that Latino male joblessness was not significant in any of the cities. This suggests that weak or nonexistent labor force attachments may affect black areas more strongly than Latino areas – a finding consistent with the notion that Latinos tend to be poor but working, while blacks are more likely to be excluded from the formal economy. Black poverty was significant in Miami and San Diego (Chapter 4 offered reasons why El Paso was the exception) and the instability index was significant in El Paso and San Diego.

Summarizing the findings regarding black homicide is even more complicated than for Latinos. There is no consistent link between immigration and black homicide, with the graphs contradicting the Poisson results in Miami and El Paso, and with specific predictors varying in their effects by location in the Poisson models. Furthermore, this study cannot explain the reason why the black homicide rate in Miami is more than twice as high than San Diego's and more than four and a half times higher than in El Paso (see Table 4.1). Still, the results showed that immigration was not positively related to black homicide in the statistical models of two out of three cities, and replications of this study for other cities may discover whether or not the situation in San Diego is an anomaly.

Ethnicity, Immigration, and Homicide: A Recap

Despite the notable variation by race, place, and over time discussed in the preceding sections, there were also consistencies in the data that warrant a review. Starting with Chapter 4, two main points emerged from the multivariate analyses:

> In five out of six regression models I found a null or negative relationship between immigration and homicide. This is perhaps the most notable finding of the study, in that it contradicts existing theories of criminal violence.

> The economic deprivation, labor market, and neighborhood instability variables were more consistently significant predictors of homicide across the models than the family structure or age variables. Although there was some variation by race and place, the stability present in the models strongly supports opportunity structure and social disorganization perspectives on black and Latino homicide in urban areas.

There were also two dominant themes in the spatial analyses from Chapter 5:

> The homicide maps of selected census tracts in each city revealed variation in the complexity of the spatial distribution of immigration and homicide rates. The maps also provided some visual support for the statistical findings from Chapter 4 (e.g., immigration was not associated

with black homicide in Miami, although it was in some tracts in San Diego).

Plotting individual homicide events disclosed no systematic relationship between immigration and "public anxiety" homicides in El Paso, and the absence of a link between Asian and black gang homicides in San Diego.

Finally, two general points can be made based on the temporal analyses:

Specific immigrant groups (e.g., Haitians in Miami and Asians in San Diego) consistently exhibited the lowest homicide rates over time in their respective cities, again casting doubt on the validity on the notion of the crime-prone immigrant.

Latino homicide rates did not track the influx of immigrants during the period of this study, but black rates did in Miami and to a lesser extent in San Diego. This suggests that future research should investigate the over-time component to immigration/homicide relationship.

In sum, the different methods I employed generally produced similar results regarding the lack of a positive relationship between immigration and homicide, and that future research should consider the spatial and temporal patterns that shape the immigration/homicide nexus.

Generalizability of the Findings

Because this study examined only three cities in the United States, there is a need to discuss whether the results are generalizable to other locations. It is difficult to say whether the major finding that immigration is not usually related to increased homicide would hold for other countries since little systematic research has been conducted on the topic. One recent study by Chapin (1997) found that immigration was positively related to crime rates (not homicide rates) in Germany, although the regression model employed was crude and did not control for poverty, instability, or other important predictors (though unemployment was included in the model). Chapin argues that the types of immigrants Germany has taken in has influenced the immigration/crime connection. In the 1950s and 1960s, immigrants were less involved in crime than natives, which the author attributes to the stable labor market ties of immigrants who were generally from European Union countries. However, by the 1980s a much larger proportion of immigrants were refugees and asylum seekers from non-European Union countries with few prospects for economic stability. It is only this recent group that appears disproportionately involved in crime. While a more sophisticated methodology, or a focus on homicide, might yield much different results in Germany, it is also possible that the findings of the present study are not applicable to international locales. Of course it is premature to claim to understand the immigration/crime link in other countries on the basis of one preliminary study of Germany.

Perhaps the more relevant question concerns the generalizability of this study to the rest of the United States. Recall that I analyzed census tract level differences in three large cities containing large numbers of recent immigrants. Since research on immigration and homicide for rural and suburban areas is scarce, due in part to the lack of sufficient numbers of immigrants in many of these areas for statistical analyses, I have no way of knowing whether my findings contradict the patterns for these kinds of locations. Thus, the present study is most applicable to other large U.S. cities with substantial immigrant populations. Initial research (not presented here) on Chicago and Houston using Poisson regression, and the same independent variables, minus the spatial lag, suggests that the findings of this study are generalizable to other large cities. My preliminary results found the following relationships between immigration and homicide:

> A significant and negative relationship for black homicide in Houston.

> A significant and negative relationship for black homicide in Chicago.

> A significant and positive relationship for Latino homicide in Houston.

> A non-significant and negative relationship for Latino homicide in Chicago.

In sum, immigration did not increase group-specific levels of homicide in these two cities, with one exception. As with the current study, the general trend suggests that immigration is generally not an important predictor of urban homicide in U.S. cities, although there are anomalies. However, much more research is needed before any definitive statements can be made about the situation in other cities.

In addition to city-by-city differences, research has also shown that predictors of homicide can vary according to the type of homicide. As but one example, in a recent city-level study Martinez (2000) found that immigration generally played a limited role in Latino homicide levels in 111 U.S. cities, after controlling for other predictors, with the exception of a positive, statistically significant relationship between immigration and homicides committed during the course of a felonious crime. A negative, statistically significant relationship was found for acquaintance killings, while no significant relationship was present for either family/intimate or stranger homicides. Since my study did not disaggregate by motivation or victim/offender relationship, I cannot say whether the results would hold for each individual homicide type.

Another open question is whether the results would hold for different time periods. Both the over-time component of the current study (i.e., the graphs in Chapter 5) and the research on Germany by Chapin (1997) imply that the effect of immigration on group-specific homicide can vary by time period. As an example, recall that while Latino homicide rates remained fairly stable over the time period of this study, the black rates displayed enormous variation. It is possible that the cross-sectional approach of this study is not capturing effects that may emerge in longitudinal research.

As I noted in endnote 15 in Chapter 2, the focus on homicide of the current study may limit its generalizability to forms of criminal violence. In fact, the "foraging model of crime" (see Hagan and Palloni, 1999:630) suggests that immigrants might be disproportionately involved in petty property crimes in order to satisfy basic subsistence needs given their sometimes tenuous connections to stable employment, while they might be less likely to commit violent crimes. But as demonstrated in Chapter 2, sociological theories of violence predict crime-facilitating effects of immigration, and popular stereotypes routinely depict violent immigrants, so empirical studies such as this one on immigration and violence are still quite useful. Of course this study is not generalizable to all types of crime, and research that would allow easy comparisons does not currently exist.

Beyond these issues, a more direct focus on the perpetrators of homicide in assessments of immigration effects would increase the generalizability of this research, especially since the social disorganization perspective has traditionally sought to explain criminal offending (Bursik and Grasmick, 1993). While the research strategy of the current study was to aggregate the location of homicide *incidents* to the tract level, other options exist to examine macrological influences on levels of offending. For example, the location of the offender's residence, counted up to the tract level, could serve as the unit of analysis since an offender may live in a different tract than where the homicide incident occurred. Or research could still focus on the location of the homicide event, except the offender (or offenders, in cases where there is more than one) would be counted. One potential problem is the quality of the information about offenders, since this is sometimes unavailable or might be based on the questionable or conflicting testimony of unreliable witnesses.

Despite the pitfalls, there is much to be gained by researching offenders. After all, it is possible that immigration increases levels of offending among Latinos and blacks even if it fails to influence or reduces victimization. That would be the case, for example, if immigrants were targeted by criminal offenders due to their lack of familiarity with or mistrust of local sources of protection and support. Additionally, conflict between recent immigrants and existing residents, which might explain the elevated levels of black victimization associated with immigration in San Diego, could increase levels of offending as well.

Implications

These potential concerns about generalizability notwithstanding, the major finding of this paper – that recent immigration does not increase community levels of homicide – has notable implications for popular and political notions of immigration as a social problem. For example, Section 1 of the controversial Proposition 187 in California declares that residents "have suffered and are suffering personal injury and damage caused by the criminal conduct of illegal aliens in this state" (cited in Butcher and Piehl 1998:457; see also Palidda, 1994, on crime and the development of anti-immigrant policies in Italy). Misleading government reports about growing numbers of immigrants in U.S. prisons provide the empirical foundations for punitive immigration laws that mandate sanctions like deportation for immigrants convicted of a crime (Hagan and Palloni, 1999; Butcher and Piehl, 1998). Such data are seized on by pseudo-academics who call for even tougher immigration laws, arguing that current policies lead "frighteningly large numbers of newcomers [to] see crime as their avenue to the American Dream" (Tanton and Lutton, 1993:217). A majority of the public seems to believe this rhetoric, as 59 percent of respondents to a 1993 *Time* magazine poll agreed that recent immigrants "add to the crime problem" (Butcher and Piehl, 1998:458).

The results of this study offer little support for claims that immigration facilitates perhaps the most serious violent crime (homicide) in three large and ethnically diverse border cities. Indeed, I argue that native groups could profit greatly from research into the counter-claim that immigration can be a stabilizing force that suppresses criminal violence. Although research on this topic is scarce, recent studies have reached a similar conclusion (cf. Martinez, 2000; Hagan and Palloni, 1999). In a cross-city study, for example, Butcher and Piehl (1998) conclude that their data provide "no support for blaming high crime rates on immigrants or immigration policy."

Similarly, Butcher and Piehl (1997) examined incarceration among immigrants and natives over two decades and concluded that immigrants had lower rates of institutionalization in correctional facilities, despite the fact that, as a group, immigrants tend to exhibit more demographic characteristics (e.g., high proportion of young, impoverished, minority males; low educational attainment) commonly associated with criminal involvement than native groups. The findings held even when disaggregated by race/ethnicity: native-born Asians, blacks, Latinos, and whites had consistently higher rates than their foreign-born counterparts. They conclude that: "if natives had the same institutionalization probabilities as immigrants, our jails and prisons would have one-third fewer inmates" (Butcher and Piehl, 1997:34).

But studies such as the one conducted by Butcher and Piehl are rare, and often not disseminated outside of the small circle of academic specialists who study immigration and crime. In the absence a research agenda that builds on this work, and communicates it in a meaningful way to policy makers and the general public, claims makers will likely continue to link immigrants with crime. The far-ranging consequences of this discourse, which reappears with each successive wave of immigrants despite its lack of empirical support (see Sellin 1938; Simon, 1985; Jaret, 1999; Hagan and Palloni 1999; Martinez and Lee 2000b), demonstrates the constitutive power of the symbolic order in shaping both the racial/ethnic identities and the social, political, and economic capital of ethnic groups (O. Lee, 1998). While power is most commonly understood in economic or political terms, there is always a symbolic, or ideological, dimension to its exercise by the dominant majority over subordinate minorities. The power to define categories of people, and the negative symbolic imagery associated with these groupings, is the necessary precursor to policies of oppression and exclusion. Lee (1998:443) argues that:

> "juridical" categories such as citizen, immigrant, African American, male, female, or "qualified" are no less the product of symbolic power than are the "disciplinary" categories of insanity, criminality, or homosexuality.

Thus, the findings presented in this book are useful not only for disputing the data on which questionable public policies are based, but also for debunking the social constructions on which these policies are premised. This kind of research reveals that policies based on "objective" data, such as the flawed government prison reports discussed above (see also Hagan and Palloni, 1999), are fundamentally ideological in nature. Indeed, Pedraza (1996a:491) persuasively argues that "the United States has yet to develop a realistic and humane immigration policy."

For example, Escobar's (1999) history of the Los Angeles Police Department's disingenuous public campaign to connect Mexicans with crime clearly shows the central role this image played in the formation of a crime-prone Mexican public identity – an identity that justified the continued subordination of this group and even ethnically motivated violence against them (e.g., the Zoot suit riot). Similarly, the symbolic force of the mythology of the "criminal immigrant" prevalent in criminological theory surely provides the ideological underpinnings of contemporary criminal justice system practices like racial profiling by law enforcement and harsh treatment by the court system. This ultimately facilitates the incarceration of disproportionate numbers of immigrants despite evidence that immigrants as a group are less crime-involved than natives (Hagan and Palloni 1999). The irony is that surveys of prisons that find the immigrants to be incarcerated at a higher rate than natives are then used as the empirical justification for increasingly draconian immigration policies, which further cement stereotypes of the criminal immigrant in the consciousness of the general public.

In addition to its relevance for issues of stereotyping and social power that affect the daily lives of disadvantaged groups of immigrants, this study also has implications for criminological theories, most notably social disorganization. At the broadest level, I concur with Bursik (2000) that ecological studies demonstrate the continued relevance of the approach Shaw and McKay (1931) popularized seventy years ago, but which has only recently begun to regain its prominence among competing perspectives. Much current work in criminology is social-psychological in orientation (Bursik, 2000), which although useful, often obscures macrological forces with the effect that crime appears to be a function of "kinds of people" rather than "kinds of places" (Bursik, 2000; Stark, 1987).

In fact, a recent Presidential Address by Farrington (2000) published in the leading criminology journal calls for more attention to the "risk factor prevention paradigm" – which although it is open to community level risk factors, has primarily focused on individual level factors that affect juveniles (e.g., "hyperactivity," poor school achievement, parental disharmony, etc.). Similarly, among symbolic interactionists crime is seen as the result of individual types (e.g., non-violent, marginally violent, violent, untra-violent persons) that dominate community interactions (Athens, 1998). By focusing on types of people, such orientations mask the impact community factors like poverty and residential instability – which are often the outcome of political struggles – on the ecological distribution of crime. In contrast, this study provides an example of the continued relevance of structural perspectives on crime, regardless of the social psychological dynamics that may also be involved.

While my research affirmed the utility of the social disorganization perspective (recall that the instability index was positive and significant in four out of six regression models), it also suggests a potential shortcoming in the classic formulation by Shaw and McKay (1969[1942]). Since the publication of their work, a common theme in the disorganization perspective has been that while immigrants are often not particularly crime-prone as a group, the community disruption wrought by immigration as a social process weakens neighborhood cohesiveness which decreases social control, thereby facilitating crime. This notion does not appear to hold in most cases in the results of this study. The strong effect of neighborhood instability on homicide, independent of the immigration variable in the statistical models, suggests that immigration may actually offer benefits to neighborhood stability, while the deleterious effects of population turnover and vacant buildings continue to exert their expected effects.

If additional research supports this finding, it may vindicate sociologists who have long argued against the "myth" (Portes, 2000:5) that residents of impoverished urban areas are poor (and victimized by criminals) because they are "disorganized" in the sense that they lack common values or strong ties to each other. While this myth may not hold for native groups, this study implies that it probably does not describe immigrant groups either.

Placed in the context of other recent studies on immigration and crime (see Hagan and Palloni 1999; Martinez and Lee 2000), the findings presented in this book support two related propositions derived from the immigration revitalization perspective (see Table 5.1) that could guide future research on immigration, ethnic heterogeneity, and crime. First, *contemporary immigration may encourage new forms of social organization that mediate the potentially crime-producing effects of the deleterious social and economic conditions found in urban neighborhoods.* These new forms of social organization may include ethnically situated informal mechanisms of social control and enclave economies that provide stable jobs to co-ethnics. In terms of ethnically situated informal mechanisms of social control, the use of shaming and stigmatization in the Little Haiti section of Miami (see Figures 5.1-5.5) is described in Adler and Clark (2003). More generally, I hypothesize that the cultural traditions of recent immigrant groups facilitate stronger family bonds and fortify parental authority to a greater degree than similarly situated native groups, a possibility that has obvious implications for effective networks of informal social control.

Turning to enclave economies, research has demonstrated the importance of ethnic-based economic networks in impoverished immigrant communities (Portes, 1997). In Miami, for example, the effect of immigration has been to stabilize and revitalize Miami's economic and cultural institutions (Portes and Stepick, 1993). Historically, African Americans in Liberty City (see Figures 5.1-5.5) have been largely excluded from enclave economies organized by immigrant groups, whereas

Haitians have established their own economic institutions in Little Haiti. The larger issue here is social capital, "the ability to gain access to resources by virtue of membership in social networks and social structure" (Portes and Rumbaut, 2001:353). Immigrants may be able to draw on a dense network of social ties, both in the United States and abroad, that are unavailable to native groups. Although impoverished, immigrant enclaves rich in social capital may adapt more effectively to the deleterious effects of economic deprivation (e.g., family disruption and crime).

The second proposition is that, regardless of the nativity of the residents, *neighborhoods may have a distinctive character, often unmeasured by variables commonly included in statistical models, that influences the relationship between structural conditions and crime.* Crutchfield, Glusker, and Bridges (1999) found a similar effect at the city level, particularly with regard to a city's historically situated niche in a changing economy, in their study of homicide in three cities. They found strong effects for education in a "high-tech city" (Seattle), both education and the presence of an underclass in an "old rust belt city" (Cleveland), and a more straightforward underclass effect in a "service sector" city (Washington, DC). These researchers have identified a "milieu effect" at the city level, an issue that has often concerned ethnographers at the neighborhood level. I argue that research in the social disorganization tradition would profit from a methodological approach, similar to Lind's (1930a; 1930b), that attempts to determine elusive qualities of "character" in high-crime, high-poverty neighborhoods.

Part of Lind's method was to document the "social atmosphere" of the slums and ghettos he analyzed. Again, the results from Figures 5.1-5.5 are informative. Although Little Haiti is not one of Miami's major tourist attractions, as it remains mired in poverty, efforts are being made to advertise it as the next "Little Havana." Stepick (1998:33) provides this description of Little Haiti:

> The Little Haiti storefronts leap out at passersby. Bright blues, reds, and oranges seem to vibrate to the pulsing Haitian music blaring from sidewalk speakers. The multilingual signs advertise distinctively Haitian products – rapid money transfer to any village in Haiti, the latest Haitian music, custom-tailored, French-styled fashions, and culinary delights such as *lambi* and *griot*. Pedestrians fill the streets. . . . [lined with] a majority of deteriorating homes. . . . For many, grass lawns have turned to dirt. Most blocks have a trash pile in front of at least one house. Cars are parked on the lawns of a few houses on each block.

Stepick's description suggests Little Haiti is a poor but lively community. Conversely, adjacent Liberty City has been described as a poor neighborhood with virtually no viable business district (Dunn, 1997). This social context may help account for the differential homicide patterns demonstrated in Figures (5.1-5.5) and has implications for areas of other cities as well.

Ethnographic research may be able to provide additional insight into the distinct social processes at work in areas in which immigrants settle that contribute to quite different social atmospheres. Perhaps this kind of analysis will discover that relative deprivation is a key variable that has gone unmeasured in quantitative work. Immigrants may compare their impoverished situation in United States to even worse conditions in their home country and may experience less strain and frustration than similarly situated minority groups (e.g., native-born African Americans), whose reference groups may include economically well-off nonLatino Whites. Because of their shared culture and history of living in a Third World country rife with political repression, it is possible that Haitian immigrants, for example, have a more optimistic outlook on their life chances in Miami than in Haiti. This outlook may also be partly a function of the enclave economies in Little Haiti and surrounding areas, discussed above, which provide at least some low-paying jobs and upward mobility for the recent arrivals.

Future Research

Having considered the substantive and theoretical significance of this book, I now provide an indication of how future research can most profitably address questions that remain incompletely answered. The most pressing need is for a replication of the results for different locations, time periods, and ethnic groups (e.g., whites, who were not included in this study). Such a replication would disclose whether the positive and significant finding between immigration and black homicide in San Diego is an aberration limited to one time period and location, or if the effect of immigration varies in some systematic manner. Of course it is also necessary to test immigration effects on racially disaggregated data sets involving other crimes. Disaggregation by crime type and victim/offender relationship would add much to our knowledge base. My hope is that the two propositions discussed above could guide this research: (1) immigration may encourage new forms of social organization that mediate disorganizing influences in inner city communities, and (2) immigration and ethnic heterogeneity may shape a neighborhood's character or social atmosphere in ways that suppress crime.

Regardless of which avenue is taken first, I argue that the use of crime maps has a great deal to offer scholars who tend to engage primarily in statistical studies of homicide (see also Weisburd and McEwen, 1997). After all, regardless of the relationship of variables like poverty or immigration to particular types of crime for a city as a whole in multivariate analyses, maps can reveal theoretically interesting exceptions to the general trend for subsections of the city. Contrasting even a small number of tracts along a few key dimensions can generate interesting propositions that may not emerge from reviewing coefficients in a regression model (cf. Lind, 1930a; 1930b). Furthermore, if a variable such as poverty is highly related to crime in the statistical models, but a map shows a high poverty area with an exceedingly low level of crime, a more in-depth study of that area using other research methods may help clarify the operative community and individual factors that work to suppress crime in one locale, but not in another (i.e., ethnography, intensive interviews, observation, etc.).

Finally, as discussed in endnote 4 in Chapter 1, future studies must explore more meaningful ways to aggregate people into categories like "immigrant" for the purposes of research. Attention to each nationality separately (e.g., Filipinos, Cambodians, Haitians, Mexicans, Cubans) or classes within a specific group (e.g., economically stable, first-wave Cubans verses less economically secure Mariel Cubans) would certainly advance our understanding of the specific impacts of immigration on crime, thus leading to further theoretical refinements. Pedraza's (1996a) typology, which classifies immigrants by *motivation for immigration* (e.g., economic vs. political) and *legal/political status* (e.g., documented, undocumented, refugee, etc.), provides an example of a potentially fruitful analytical framework, as does the concept of *segmented assimilation* discussed in Chapter 4. Another issue concerns the generational and nativity status of immigrant populations: whether they are first-generation immigrants born abroad, or part of the second and third generations born in the United States. This study focused on those born abroad who entered this country during 1980-1990, as measured by the "year of entry" census variable. As such, it was unable to assess the impact of subsequent generations, as well as illegal immigrants.

Implementing strategies designed to address these concerns will no doubt require considerable creativity if existing data sets are used – as these tend not to make fine distinctions by ethnicity or immigration status – or time-consuming and expensive data collection. Gathering this information usually requires direct access to detailed case files with personal identifiers and lengthy narratives that provide extensive information on victims and offenders. Despite labor-intensive nature of working with such original data, the potential benefits of this kind of research to criminologists and immigration researchers, and potentially policy makers, are quite substantial.

In conclusion, this study provided a quantitative and qualitative evaluation of claims about immigration and crime – claims which have significant consequences for both immigrants and natives. My findings suggest that future research along these lines has much to offer criminological theory, public policy, and perhaps most importantly, popular understandings of the complex relationship between immigration and crime. But in the end, I also agree with Hagan and Palloni (1998:382) that researchers should:

> place the priority on finding ways to preserve, protect, and promote the social capital that... immigrants bring to their experience in the United States, rather than overemphasize issues of crime and punishment.

Academic study of immigrants that is limited to topics like gangs and crime, the current favorites among researchers, can only serve to promote the impression that immigrants are a crime-prone group – an image that the empirical research of the last 100 years (see Martinez and Lee, 2000b; Mears, 2001; T. Waters, 1999), including this book, does not support.

Endnotes

1. According to figures compiled by the Immigration and Naturalization Service (1987), San Diego, El Paso, and Miami ranked first, second, and nineteenth, respectively, in admissions to the United States in 1986, relative to all other points of entry. A city such as Miami can be considered on the "border" because it serves as a major port of entry and final destination for immigrants, even if it is not physically located next to a foreign country, as with El Paso and San Diego.

2. Although reference to the "post-1965 wave," sometimes referred to as the "fourth wave" (Pedraza, 1996b), of immigrants has received criticism among scholars who point out that groups such as Latinos immigrated in large numbers prior to the immigration law reforms in 1965, others point out that the shift in immigration patterns over the last four decades is in many ways tied to these reforms (especially in the case of Asians) and the social and political changes that occurred in this period (e.g., the civil rights movement, see Kibria, 2002). One thing is certain: the latest wave of immigrants is no longer primarily European in origin. Rather, they tend to come from Latin American, Asian, and Caribbean countries (Kibria, 2002; Pedraza, 1996b). In terms of the cities studied in this book, Rumbaut (1992:282) points to "the large increase in the Mexican-origin population in California" associated with the Bracero Program from 1942 to 1964, relevant for San Diego and El Paso; the impact of the 1965 Immigration Act, which "eliminated racist quotas barring Asians" (p. 280), directly affecting San Diego; and the wave of Cuban exiles that "began in earnest" (p.284) in 1960, forever changing the ethnic composition in Miami. More generally, Rumbaut (1992) notes that the 1980 Census reported that among the foreign-born, 87.4% of Asians, 68.6% of Mexicans, and 87.2% of Cubans entered the U.S. between 1960 and 1980. For these reasons, this book occasionally references the commonly used 1965 date in order to draw attention to the consequences of these historical shifts, while recognizing that the use of a single year to demarcate complex social trends is always subject to debate.

135

3. Lamm and Imhoff (1985) are a classic example as they rely on second- and third-hand impressions, rather than systematically collected, verifiable evidence, to support their claims of immigrants as a crime-prone group. They base their contention that "there is good evidence that 40 percent of [Mariel immigrants in Miami] were criminals or had histories of criminal behavior or of mental illness" (p. 49) almost exclusively on the questionable testimony of a Harrisburg, Pennsylvania police detective. This detective suggests that "the real figure is much, much higher" (p. 62-3) and describes the source of his information in phrases like "this guy told me" (p. 63) and that another law enforcement official "told me he had talked to some people, heard some things" (p. 70).

4. Principles of "network analysis" point to the danger inherent in aggregating persons with similar characteristics into social categories (e.g., "immigrants") without considering the concrete relationships among them (see Wellman, 1983). Upon empirical examination, such categories may group together structurally isolated individuals or groups who may turn out to have very little in common. In this sense, "immigrant" appears to be a wastebasket term, as Portes and Stepick (1985) demonstrate in their study of the differential quality of ties to "enclave economies" of Mariel and Haitian immigrants in Miami. Thus, network analysis argues for an examination not of categories of people, but of the effect of the concrete structural links that embed people in social relationships and constitute "social capital" (Portes and Sensenbrenner, 1993). Social disorganization, according to this view, is related to the quality of ties in a community, not to the presence or absence of "immigrants." Thomas, Park, and Miller (1966[1921]:183) make a related point that:

> in all groups certain individuals resemble individuals in other groups more than they resemble the average member of their own group.... Certainly the difference between an intellectual Pole and a Polish peasant is as profound as possible.

On the other hand, labels such as "Latino" and "immigrant" continue to guide research because non-white groups generally experience social conditions (e.g., poverty) to a greater degree than the dominant white majority. Regarding the focus of the current study, because research has found that whites, blacks, and Latinos exhibit vastly different levels of homicide (Martinez and Lee, 1999) it makes empirical sense to explore the conditions that lead to these group differences. Furthermore, since popular and scholarly notions about immigrants and crime make few of the nuanced distinctions suggested by network theorists, investigating claims on their own terms seems a useful first step in crafting a long-term violence research agenda that encompasses various immigrant groups.

5. This is not to suggest that sociological approaches to the study of crime, and the ecological variant in particular, are without problems (see Einstadter and Henry, 1995). A common criticism of ecological explanations concerns the issue of spurious results. Specifically, homicide is an act most often carried out by a single individual, and studies that draw conclusions about individual behavior from aggregate data (e.g., neighborhood levels of poverty) commit the "ecological fallacy." This has led some scholars to direct more attention to the types of individuals present in communities, rather than the structural characteristics of the communities themselves (cf. Athens, 1998). In addition, ecological studies tend to infer causality from correlational methods, and concepts like "social disorganization" are often tautological (i.e., acting as both a description of a condition and its cause). Still, homicides are not randomly distributed throughout urban areas, and the ecological approach is well-suited to understanding this distribution, as long as one is cognizant of the issues discussed above.

6. Thomas, Park, and Miller (1966[1921]:197-98) were especially concerned about the threats to democracy and "self-preservation" of importing culturally inferior groups:

> If visitors are disorderly, unsanitary, or ignorant, the group which incorporates them, even temporarily, will not escape the bad effects of this. Every country has a certain amount of culturally undeveloped material. We have it, for instance, in the Negroes and Indians, the Southern mountaineers, the Mexicans and Spanish-Americans, and the slums. There is a limit, however, to the amount of material of this kind that a country can incorporate without losing the character of its culture.... if we should receive, say, a million Congo blacks and a million Chinese coolies annually, and if they should propagate faster than the white Americans, it is certain that our educational system would break down; we could not even impart the "three R's." We should then be in a state of chaos

unless we abandoned the idea of democracy and secured efficiency by reverting to the "ordering and forbidding" type of state.... [Immigrants] cannot be intelligent citizens unless they "get the hang" of American ways of thinking as well as doing.

Foreshadowing contemporary fears (see Lamm and Imhoff, 1985), Thomas, Park, and Miller (1966[1921]:202,207) advocated that immigrants be forced to "speak the language of the country" in order to facilitate a speedy assimilation and argued that "the organization of the immigrant community is necessary as a regulative measure." Again, this overriding concern with the social control of immigrants and ethnic minorities derived from the ethnicity theorists' beliefs that "when uncivilized races come into contact with the products of our civilization they appropriate the vices and ornaments, the whisky and beads, and leave the more substantial values" (p. 207) and that "the amount of immigration which we can continue to tolerate or encourage depends on their character" (p. 206).

7. While much attention has been focused on black/white differences in homicide, intragroup comparisons of black homicides have not been as prominent. In many cases, within-group differences are larger than intergroup differences and an exclusive concern with the latter paints a distorted picture of the race/homicide relationship (Hawkins, 1999a).

8. Escobar (1999:120) found that studies conducted by law enforcement agencies painted "a rather sympathetic picture" of Mexican criminality in the pre-WWII United States, which contrasted sharply with the stereotypical views of the criminally inclined Mexican commonly held by law enforcement officers. In fact, academic studies also "found that Mexicans were not particularly inclined toward criminality" (Escobar, 1999:105).

9. Jaret (1999:10) calls Brimelow's book the "classic text" of the post-1965 wave of immigration and compares it to the "classic" of the earlier period, Madison Grant's (1916) *The Passing of the Great Race.* He notes that both books fuse "nativist fears and accusations with racist notions of white supremacy" (Jaret, 1999:10).

10. Shaw and McKay (1969[1942]) found that over several decades the most recent immigrant groups, along with native blacks, consistently accounted for the highest proportion of delinquency in

Chicago. Yet this relationship was spurious because as a given immigrant group moved out of high delinquency areas the rates of delinquency among their children dropped substantially. Thus, "factors of race, nativity, and nationality are [not] vitally related to the problem of juvenile delinquency" (p. 162). Rather, "within the same type of social area, the foreign born and the natives, recent immigrant nationalities, and older immigrants produce very similar rates of delinquents" (p. 160). That delinquency was a function of physical distribution across the "natural areas" of the city, not race or ethnicity, can be seen in the striking within-group variations in delinquency rates (see p. 159). For example, area rates for foreign-born children ranged from 0.53 to 15.45 per hundred, while native white children's rates exhibited almost exactly the same range (0.48 to 14.94).

11. In a polemic arguing for a restriction of immigration titled "Our Anti-Social Mexican Class," Carl May (1929, as cited in Escobar, 1999:113) foreshadowed Merton's hypothesis when he suggested:

> Members of the present Mexican generation believe they, like others, are entitled to recreation and pleasure; and that if they cannot obtain it legitimately, they will resort to criminal acts to satisfy their desires.

Lamm and Imhoff (1985:53) provide a more contemporary application of anomie theory by justifying their undocumented contention that immigrants throughout the world must be disproportionately involved in crime with the following rationale:

> Immigrants, after all, are displaced persons; many avenues of success in their new societies will be closed to them.... and they will encounter discrimination which could engender resentment and ill will toward their new country.

Lamm and Imhoff (1985:46) also cite the 1978 U.S. House Select Committee on Population, which argued that illegal immigrants might:

> ...become wedged into an inferior status, part of a substratum in American society that is outside the education and social systems.... [Their children] will think of themselves as Americans with rising expectations and dreams of upward mobility.... Continued illegal immigration may in time

produce a second generation of alienated, frustrated young
people in our society, capable of producing hostilities,
disturbances, and protests like those of the 1960's.

12. One chapter from the Wickersham Commission's report on Crime
and the Foreign Born maintained that crimes of violence "were
common among Mexicans not because they are Mexicans, but because
they live in a certain cultural stage, where fighting is approved..."
(Handman, 1931:256)

13. In this vein, arrest statistics compiled by the LAPD in the 1930s
found that Mexicans were over-represented for liquor-law violations, a
result that Escobar (1999:129) attributes to the criminalization of
"activities [i.e., drinking] that Mexicans considered lawful and part of
normal everyday life."

14. Disorganization has long been used to explain not only the higher
crime rates present in communities in which immigrants settle, but also
the more widespread criminality of the immigrants themselves.
Handman (1931:258) argued that crimes of Mexicans living in the
United States were a function of:

> the nomadic life which [they] are leading and with the
> dislocation and disorganization that takes place within a
> person who is torn from his village community with its system
> of control and plunged into a new and strange and, in the
> main, disorganized environment.

Lamm and Imhoff (1985:76-7) offer more extreme view of the
disorganizing effects of immigration, a view where agreement about
norms is impossible and community control breaks down to a point
where the whole society becomes "splintered":

> Let me say it directly: massive immigration involves profound
> social and cultural dangers.... there are certain universal
> pathologies that characterize the fall of history's civilizations.
> Ethnic, racial, and religious differences can become such a
> pathology; they can grow and fester, and eventually splinter a
> society.

15. One potential criticism of this study is its reliance on homicide as a proxy for "crime." Some scholars have argued that immigrants are more likely to be over-represented in drug or property crimes, and possibly less involved in violent crimes. For example, Hagan and Palloni (1999:630) discuss the notion that immigrant offending follows the "foraging model of crime" – the commission of petty property crimes in order to satisfy subsistence needs until a legitimate source of income can be secured. However, studying the immigrant/homicide relationship is still useful for at least three reasons. First, data on community levels of petty theft are notoriously unreliable, and reflect reporting and enforcement behavior rather than the actual levels of theft. On the other hand, virtually all homicides eventually become known to police, thus allowing for accurate measurement of the dependent variable. Second, popular claims about crime-prone immigrants usually do not distinguish between types of crime, and in fact often emphasize exceptionally violent incidents (cf. Lamm and Imhoff, 1985). And third, the prominent sociological theories reviewed in this chapter propose to explain both violent and non-violent crime and have long been used to account for variation in homicide levels across communities.

16. Both popular and scholarly ideas about immigration work in concert to provide the foundation for immigration policies, both in the United States and elsewhere. For example, racist notions about the potential ability of certain groups of immigrants to "integrate" into society continue to guide the bureaucratic processing of immigrants' family reunification applications in Austria (Van Leeuwen and Wodak, 1999). Taken-for-granted stereotypes (supported by sociological theories) provide a discursive resource in the formal explanations for rejections offered by government workers, in the absence of empirical evidence on the integration (or lack thereof) of immigrants into Austrian society. This latest round of discrimination is particularly interesting because, like the United States, Austria has historically been a destination point for diverse immigrant groups.

17. Census tracts are smaller than what residents might define as "neighborhoods." But aggregating tracts into neighborhoods would yield too few units for multivariate analysis in Miami and El Paso, so the tract level is the closest one can get to modeling "natural areas" of cities. One advantage of tracts is that they capture within-

neighborhood variation, yet remain more homogeneous than larger aggregates such as cities or counties.

18. Counts of homicide events were collected from internal police files and are discussed in more detail in the Data Collection section of this chapter. Tract-level population characteristics were taken from the 1990 census (STF3A).

19. However, recent work on nonimmigrant black ghettos has found that homogeneous areas are not better organized for social control (Anderson, 1990), and suffer from the concentration of multiple social problems (Sampson and Wilson, 1995).

20. The Miami and San Diego data were collected from police files by Dr. Ramiro Martinez, Jr., between 1994 and 1998. El Paso police files were provided by S. Fernando Rodriguez. I participated in the collection of supplemental materials from the Medical Examiner's office in Miami. All data were coded and cleaned by this author and Dr. Martinez, with the assistance of several undergraduate assistants. I verified the accuracy of all files on which undergraduates worked.

21. While homicide event counts were used in the Poisson models, rates were better suited for the visual presentation in this chapter. The tracts were chosen, in part, for their large populations; as a result, the rates displayed in the maps are not biased by a small denominator in the calculation. Note that rates are per 10,000 residents as measured by the 1990 census and average over the ten-year time period.

22. It is important that several tracts on the lower right (west) side of the map with virtually no black homicides – despite often substantial numbers of black residents (e.g., tract 3208 has 1,626 black residents) – exhibit low black poverty. This finding supports Hawkins' (1999a) arguments about the need for increased attention to within-group differences as they manifest across locations with distinct social characteristics. Media presentations often ignore this diversity, thus giving the impression that urban homicide is a "black" problem, as opposed to a problem of location or social class (Hawkins, 1999a).

23. I used population estimates appearing in the Federal Bureau of Investigation's (1980-1995) Uniform Crime Reports for the city-wide rates that appear in the Figures; immigrant counts are from the Immigration and Naturalization Service (1997; 1987).

References

Abbott, Edith. 1931. "The Problem of Crime and the Foreign Born."
  Pp. 23-69 in National Commission on Law Observance and
  Enforcement (ed.). *Report on Crime and the Foreign Born,
  No. 10.* Washington, D.C.: U.S. Government Printing
  Office.

Adler, Emily Stier and Roger Clark. 2003. *How It's Done: An
  Invitation to Social Research*, 2nd ed. Belmont, CA:
  Wadsworth.

Aguirre, Adalberto, and Jonathan H. Turner. 1998. *American Ethnicity:
  The Dynamics and Consequences of Discrimination.* Boston:
  McGraw-Hill.

Alaniz, Maria Luisa, Randi S. Cartmill, and Robert Nash Parker. 1998.
  "Immigrants and Violence: The Importance of Neighborhood
  Context." *Hispanic Journal of Behavioral Sciences* 20:155-74.

Alba, Richard D., John R. Logan, and Paul E. Bellair. 1994. "Living
  With Crime: The Implications of Racial/Ethnic Differences in
  Suburban Location." *Social Forces* 73:395-434.

Alba, Richard D., and Victor Nee. 1997. "Rethinking Assimilation
  Theory for a New Era of Immigration." *International
  Migration Review* 31:826-874.

Anderson, Elijah. 1990. *Streetwise: Race, Class, and Change in an
  Urban Community.* Chicago: University of Chicago Press.

Anderson, Elijah. 1999. *Code of the Street: Decency, Violence, and the
  Moral Life of the Inner City.* New York: W. W. Norton.

Anselin, Luc. 1995. *SpaceStat: A Software Program for the Analysis of
  Spatial Data, Version 1.80.* Morgantown, WV: Regional
  Research Institute, West Virginia University.

Anselin, Luc, Jacqueline Cohen, David Cook, Wilpen Gorr, and
  George Tita. 2000. "Spatial Analyses of Crime." In David
  Dunfee (ed.). *Criminal Justice 2000, Volume 4.* Washington
  DC: National Institute of Justice.

Athens, Lonnie. 1998. "Dominance, Ghettos, and Violent Crime." *The
  Sociological Quarterly* 39:673-91.

Avakame, Edem F. 1998. "How Different Is Violence in the Home? An Examination of Some Correlates of Stranger and Intimate Homicide." *Criminology* 36:601-32.

Balkwell, James W. 1990. "Ethnic Inequality and the Rate of Homicide." *Social Forces* 69:53-70.

Bankston, Carl L. III. 1998. "Youth Gangs and the New Second Generation: A Review Essay." *Aggression and Violent Behavior* 3:35-45.

Biblarz, Timothy J., and Adrian E. Raftery. 1999. "Family Structure, Educational Attainment, and Socioeconomic Success: Rethinking the 'Pathology of Matriarchy.'" *American Journal of Sociology* 105:321-365.

Block, Carolyn Rebecca. 1993. "Lethal Violence in the Chicago Latino Community." Pp. 267-342 in Anna Victoria Wilson (ed.). *Homicide: The Victim/Offender Connection.* Cincinnati, OH: Anderson.

Brimelow, Peter J. 1996. *Alien Nation.* New York, NY: Random House.

Bourgois, Philippe. 1995. *In Search of Respect: Selling Crack in El Barrio.* Cambridge: Cambridge University Press.

Bursik, Robert J., Jr. 1988. "Social Disorganization and Theories of Crime and Delinquency: Problems and Prospects." *Criminology* 26:519-51.

Bursik, Robert J., Jr. 2000. "The Systemic Theory of Neighborhood Crime Rates." Pp. 87-103 in Sally S. Simpson (ed.). *Of Crime and Criminality.* Thousand Oaks, CA: Pine Forge Press.

Bursik, Robert J., Jr., and Harold G. Grasmick. 1993. "Economic Deprivation and Neighborhood Crime Rates, 1960-1980." *Law and Society Review* 27:263-83.

Butcher, Kristin F., and Anne Morrison Piehl. 1997. "Recent Immigrants: Unexpected Implications for Crime and Incarceration." NBER Working Paper 6067. Cambridge, MA: National Bureau of Economic Research.

Butcher, Kristin F., and Anne Morrison Piehl. 1998. "Cross City Evidence on the Relationship between Immigration and Crime." *Journal of Policy Analysis and Management* 17:457-93.

Cameron, A. Colin, and Trivedi, Pravin K. 1986. *Regression Analysis of Count Data.* Cambridge: Cambridge University Press.

Carino, Benjamin V. "Filipino Americans: Many and Varied." Pp. 293-301 in Silvia Pedraza and Ruben G. Rumbaut (eds.). *Origins and Destinies: Immigration, Race, and Ethnicity in America.* Belmont, CA: Wadsworth.

Chapin, Wesley D. 1997. "Auslander Raus? The Empirical Relationship between Immigration and Crime in Germany." *Social Science Quarterly* 78:543-58.

Cliff, Andrew David, and J. Keith Ord. 1981. *SpatialProcesses: Models and Applications.* London: Pion.

Cloward, Richard, and Lloyd Ohlin. 1960. *Delinquency and Opportunity: A Theory of Delinquent Gangs.* New York: The Free Press.

Corcoran, M. 1995. "Rags to Rags: Poverty and Mobility in the United States." *Annual Review of Sociology* 21:237-267.

Crutchfield, Robert D. 1989. "Labor Stratification and Violent Crime." *Social Forces* 68:489-512.

Crutchfield, Robert D., Ann Glusker, and George S. Bridges. 1999. "A Tale of Three Cities: Labor Markets and Homicide." *Sociological Focus* 32:65-83.

Crutchfield, Robert D., and Susan R. Pitchford. 1997. "Work and Crime: The Effects of Labor Stratification." *Social Forces* 76:93-118.

Dunn, Marvin. 1997. *Black Miami in the Twentieth Century.* Gainsville: University Press of Florida.

Edin, Kathyrn. 2000. "What Do Low-Income Single Mothers Say about Marriage?" *SocialProblems* 47:112-133.

Einstadter, Werner, and Stuart Henry. 1995. *Criminological Theory: An Analysis of Its Underlying Assumptions.* New York: Harcourt Brace.

Escobar, Edward J. 1999. *Race, Police, and the Making of a* Political Identity: Mexican Americans and the Los *Angeles Police Department, 1900-1945.* Berkeley, CA: University of California Press.

Espiritu, Len Le. 1995. *Filipino American Lives.* Philadelphia: Temple University Press.

Farrington, David P. 2000. "Explaining and Preventing Crime: The Globalization of Knowledge — The American Society of Criminology 1999 Presidential Address." *Criminology* 38:1-24.

Federal Bureau of Investigation. 1980-1995. *Uniform Crime Reports.* Washington, DC: U.S. Government Printing Office.

Ferracuti, Franco. 1968. "European Migration and Crime." Pp. 189-219 in Marvin E. Wolfgang (ed.). *Crime and Culture: Essays in Honor of Thorsten Sellin*. New York: John Wiley & Sons.

Fienberg, Stephen E. 1984. *The Analysis of Cross-Classified Categorical Data*. Cambridge, MA: MIT Press.

Flewelling, Robert L. and Kirk R. Williams. 1999. "Categorizing Homicides: The Use of Disaggregated Data in Homicide Research." Pp. 96-106 in M. Dwayne Smith and Margaret A. Zahn (eds.). *Homicide: A Sourcebook of Social Research*. Thousand Oaks, CA: Sage.

Flint, Colin. 1998. "To Explain or Understand Evil: Comparing Hermeneutic and Rational Choice Approaches to the Analysis of Nazism: A Review." *Social Science Quarterly* 79:466-74.

Fox, James Alan, and Marianne W. Zawitz. 2000. *Homicide Trends in the United States*. Washington DC: Bureau of Justice Statistics.

Garcia, M.C. 1996. *Havana USA: Cuban Exiles and Cuban Americans in South Florida, 1959-1994*. Berkeley, CA: University of California Press.

Gardner, William, Edward P. Mulvey, and Esther C. Shaw. 1995. "Regression Analyses of Counts and Rates: Poisson, Overdispersed Poisson, and Negative Binomial." *Psychological Bulletin* 118:392-405.

Gilligan, James. 1997. *Violence: Reflections on a National Epidemic*. New York: Vintage.

Gonzales, Adolfo. 1996. *Historical Case Study: San Diego and Tijuana Border Region Relationship with the San Diego Police Department, 1957-1994*. Ann Arbor: UMI Dissertation Services.

Gordon, Robert A. 1967. "Issues in the Ecological Study of Delinquency." *American Sociological Review* 32:927-44.

Grenier, Guillermo J., and Lisandro Perez. 1996. "Miami Spice: The Ethnic Cauldron Simmers." Pp. 360-372 in Silvia Pedraza and Ruben G. Rumbaut (eds.). *Origins and Destinies: Immigration, Race, and Ethnicity in America*. Belmont, CA: Wadsworth.

Gurr, Ted Robbert. 1989. "The History of Violent Crime in America," Pp. 11-20 in Ted Robert Gurr (ed.). *Violence in America, Volume 1*. Newbury Park, CA: Sage.

Hagan, John, and Alberto Palloni. 1998. "Immigration and Crime in the United States," Pp. 367-87 in James P. Smith and Barry Edmonston (eds.). *The Immigration Debate*. Washington, D.C.: National Academy Press.

Hagan, John, and Alberto Palloni. 1999. "Sociological Criminology and the Mythology of Hispanic Immigration and Crime." *Social Problems* 46:617-32.

Handman, Max Sylvius. 1931. "Preliminary Report on Nationality and Delinquency: The Mexican in Texas." Pp. 245-64 in National Commission on Law Observance and Enforcement (ed.). *Report on Crime and the Foreign Born, No. 10*. Washington, D.C.: U.S. Government Printing Office.

Harris, David A. 2002. *Profiles in Injustice: Why Racial Profiling Cannot Work*. New York: New Press.

Hawkins, Darnell F. 1999a. "African Americans and Homicide." Pp. 195-210 in M. Dwayne Smith and Margaret A. Zahn (eds.). *Homicide: A Sourcebook of Social Research*. Thousand Oaks, CA: Sage.

Hawkins, Darnell F. 1999b. "Race and Ethnicity." Pp. 1-6 in Ronald Gottesman (ed.). *Violence in America: An Encyclopedia, Volume 3*. New York: Charles Scribner's Sons.

Hayner, Norman S. 1937. "Delinquency Areas in the Puget Sound Region." *American Journal of Sociology* 39:314-28.

Heitgerd, Janet L., and Robert J. Bursik, Jr. 1987. "Extracommunity Dynamics and the Ecology of Delinquency." *American Journal of Sociology* 92:775-87

Hunt, Matthew O. 2000. "Status, Religion, and the 'Belief in a Just World': Comparing African Americans, Latinos, and Whites." *Social Science Quarterly* 81:325-343.

Immigration and Naturalization Service. 1987. *Statistical Yearbook of the Immigration and Naturalization Service, 1986*. Washington, DC: U.S. Government Printing Office.

Immigration and Naturalization Service. 1997. *Statistical Yearbook of the Immigration and Naturalization Service, 1996*. Washington, DC: U.S. Government Printing Office.

James, Winston. 2002. "Explaining Afto-Caribbean Social Mobility in the United States: Beyond the Sowell Thesis." *Comparative Studies in Society and History* 44:218-262.

Jaret, Charles. 1999. "Troubled by Newcomers: Anti-Immigrant Attitudes and Action During Two Eras of Mass Immigration to the United States." *Journal of American Ethnic History* 18:9-39.

Katz, Jack. 1988. *Seductions of Crime: Moral and Sensual Attractions of Doing Evil*. New York: HarperCollins.

Kibria, Nazli. 2002. *Becoming Asian American: Second Generation Chinese and Korean American Identities*. Baltimore: Johns Hopkins University Press.

Kohfeld, Carol W., and John Sprague. 1988. "Urban Unemployment Drives Urban Crime." *Urban Affairs Quarterly* 24:215-41.

LaFree, Gary. 1999. *Losing Legitimacy: Street Crime and the Decline of Social Institutions*. Boulder, CO: Westview Press.

LaFree, Gary, Robert J. Bursik, Jr., James Short, and Ralph B. Taylor. 2000. "The Changing Nature of Crime in America." Pp. 1-49 in Gary LaFree (ed.). *Criminal Justice 2000: The Changing Nature of Crime, Volume 1*. Washington DC: National Institute of Justice.

Lambert, John R. 1970. *Crime, Police, and Race Relations: A Study in Birmingham*. London: Oxford University Press.

Lamm, Richard D., and Gary Imhoff. 1985. *The Immigration Time Bomb: The Fragmenting of America*. New York: Truman Talley.

Land, Kenneth C., and Glenn Deane. 1992. "On the Large Sample Estimation of Regression Models with Spatial-or Network-Effects Terms: A Two-Stage Least Squares Approach." *Sociological Theory* 22:221-248.

Land, Kenneth C., Paricia L. McCall, and Lawrence E. Cohen. 1990. "Structural Covariates of Homicide Rates: Are There Any Invariances Across Time and Space?" *American Journal of Sociology* 95:922-63.

Lane, Roger. 1986. *Roots of Violence in Black Philadelphia, 1860-1900*. Cambridge, MA: Harvard University Press.

Lane, Roger. 1989. "On the Social Meaning of Homicide Trends in America. Pp. 55-79 in Ted Robert Gurr (ed.). *Violence in America, Volume 1*. Newbury Park, CA: Sage.

Lee, Matthew R. 2000. "Concentrated Poverty, Race, and Homicide." *The Sociological Quarterly* 41:189-206.

Lee, Matthew T. 2000. "Ethnicity, Immigration, and Homicide on the Border: A Comparison of El Paso, Miami, and San Diego (1985-1995)." Ph.D. Dissertation, University of Delaware.

Lee, Matthew T., and Ramiro Martinez, Jr. 1999. "Symbolic Violence." Pp. 246-52 in Ronald Gottesman (ed.). *Violence in America: An Encyclopedia, Volume 3*. New York: Charles Scribner's Sons.

Lee, Matthew T., and Ramiro Martinez, Jr. 2002. "Social Disorganization Revisited: Mapping the Recent Immigration and Black Homicide Relationship in Northern Miami." *Sociological Focus* 35:363-380.

Lee, Matthew T., Ramiro Martinez, Jr., and S. Fernando Rodriguez. 2000. "Contrasting Latino Homicide: The Victim and Offender Relationship in El Paso and Miami." *Social Science Quarterly* 81:375-88.

Lee, Matthew T., Ramiro Martinez, Jr., and Richard B. Rosenfeld. 2001. "Does Immigration Increase Homicide?: Negative Evidence From Three Border Cities." *The Sociological Quarterly* 42:559-580.

Lee, Orville. 1998. "Culture and Democratic Theory: Toward a Theory of Symbolic Democracy." *Constellations* 5:399-455.

Lee, Yoon Ho. 1998. "Acculturation and Delinquent Behavior: The Case of Korean American Youths." *International Journal of Comparative and Applied Criminal Justice.* 22:273-92.

Lewis, Oscar. 1965. *La Vida: A Puerto Rican Family in the Culture of Poverty.* New York: Random House.

Lilly, J. Robert, Francis T. Cullen, and Richard A. Ball. 1989. *Criminological Theory: Context and Consequences.* Newbury Park, CA: Sage.

Lind, Andrew W. 1930a. "Some Ecological Patterns of Community Disorganization in Honolulu." *American Journal of Sociology* 36:206-20.

Lind, Andrew W. 1930b. "The Ghetto and the Slum." *Social Forces* 9:206-15.

Linton, April. 2002. "Immigration and the Structure of Demand: Do Immigrants Alter the Labor Market Composition of U.S. Cities?" *International Migration Review* 36:58-80.

Logan, John R., Richard D. Alba, Michael Dill, and Min Zhou. 2000. "Ethnic Segmentation in the American Metropolis: Increasing Divergence in Economic Incorporation, 1980-1990." *International Migration Review* 34:98-132.

Logan, John R., Richard D. Alba, and Thomas McNulty. 1994. "Ethnic Economies in Metropolitan Regions: Miami and Beyond." *Social Forces* 72:691-724.

Logan, John R., and Brian J. Stults. 1999. "Racial Differences in Exposure to Crime: The City and the Suburbs of Cleveland in 1990." *Criminology* 37:215-76.

Lutton, Wayne. 1996. "Immigration and Crime." Pp. 95-108 in John
    Tanton, Denis McCormack, and Joseph Wayne Smith (eds.).
    *Immigration and the Social Contract: The Implosion of
    Western Societies*. Aldershot, England: Avebury.

Martinez, Ramiro, Jr. 1997. "Homicide Among the 1980 Mariel
    Refugees in Miami: Victims and Offenders." *Hispanic
    Journal of Behavioral Sciences* 19:107-122.

Martinez, Ramiro, Jr. 2000. "Immigration and Urban Violence: The
    Link Between Immigrant Latinos and Types of Homicide."
    Social Science Quarterly 81:363-374.

Martinez, Ramiro, Jr. 2002. *Latino Homicide: Immigration, Violence,
    and Community*. New York: Routledge.

Martinez, Ramiro, Jr., and Matthew T. Lee. 1998. "Immigration and the
    Ethnic Distribution of Homicide." *Homicide Studies* 2:291-
    304.

Martinez, Ramiro, Jr., and Matthew T. Lee. 1999. "Extending Ethnicity
    in Homicide Research: The Case of Latinos." Pp. 211-20 in
    M. Dwayne Smith and Margaret A. Zahn (eds.). *Homicide: A
    Sourcebook of Social Research*. Thousand Oaks, CA: Sage.

Martinez, Ramiro, Jr., and Matthew T. Lee. 2000a. "Comparing the
    Context of Immigrant Homicides in Miami: Haitians,
    Jamaicans, and Mariels." *International Migration Review*,
    34:793-811.

Martinez, Ramiro, Jr., and Matthew T. Lee. 2000b. "On Immigration
    and Crime." In Gary LaFree and Robert J. Bursik, Jr. (eds.)
    *Criminal Justice 2000: The Changing Nature of Crime,
    Volume 1*. Washington DC: National Institute of Justice.

Massey, Douglas S. 1995. "Getting Away With Murder: Segregation
    and Violent Crime in America." *University of Pennsylvania
    Law Review* 143:1203-1232.

McWilliams, John C. 1990. *The Protectors: Harry J. Anslinger and the
    Federal Bureau of Narcotics, 1930-1962*. Newark: University
    of Delaware Press.

Mears, Daniel P. 2001. "The Immigration-Crime Nexus: Toward and
    Analytic Framework for Assessing and Guiding Theory,
    Research, and Policy." *Sociological Perspectives* 44:1-19.

Merton, Robert K. 1938. "Social Structure and Anomie." *American
    Sociological Review* 3:672-82.

Messner, Steven F., and Richard Rosenfeld. 1997. *Crime and the
    American Dream*. Belmont, CA: Wadsworth.

Messner, Steven F., and Kenneth Tardiff. 1986. "Economic Inequality and Levels of Homicide: An Analysis of Urban Neighborhoods." *Criminology* 24:297-317.

Mizell, C. Andre. 1999. "Life Course Influences on African American Men's Depression: Adolescent Parental Composition, Self-Concept, and Adult Earnings." *Journal of Black Studies* 29:467-490.

Morenoff, Jeffrey D., and Robert J. Sampson. 1997. "Violent Crime and the Spatial Dynamics of Neighborhood Transition: Chicago, 1970-1990." *Social Forces* 76:31-64.

Musolf, Gil Richard. 1998. *Structure and Agency in Everyday Life: An Introduction to Social Psychology.* Dix Hills, NY: General Hall.

National Consortium on Violence Research (NCOVR). 2000. "A Research Program for Better Understanding the Role of Race/Ethnicity in Violence." Unpublished paper.

National Public Radio (NPR). 2001. "Census and the Cities." *Talk of the Nation*, March 28. Transcript available from www.npr.org.

Nettler, Gwynn. 1984. *Explaining Crime.* New York: McGraw Hill.

Nevins, Joseph. 2002. *Operation Gatekeeper: The Rise of the "Illegal Alien" and the Making of the U.S. Mexico Boundary.* Routledge. New York.

Ong, Paul, and John M. Liu. 1994. "U.S. Immigration Policies and Asian Migration." Pp. 45-73 in Paul Ong, Edna Bonacich, and Lucie Cheng (eds.). *The New Asian Immigration in Los Angeles and Global Restructuring.* Philadelphia: Temple University Press.

Osgood, D. Wayne. 2000. "Poisson-Based Regression Analysis of Aggregate Crime Rates." *Journal of Quantitative Criminology* 16:21-43.

Ousey, Graham. 1999. "Homicide, Structural Factors, and the Racial Invariance Assumption." *Criminology* 37:405-26.

Palidda, Salvatore. 1994. "Deviance and Criminality among Immigrants: Some Hypotheses for Sociological Research." *Inchiesta* 24:25-39.

Park, Robert E. 1925a. "Community Organization and Juvenile Delinquency." Pp. 99-112 in Robert E. Park, Ernest W. Burgess, and Roderick D. McKenzie (eds.) *The City.* Chicago: University of Chicago Press.

Park, Robert E. 1925b. "Community Organization and the Romantic Temper." Pp. 113-22 in Robert E. Park, Ernest W. Burgess, and Roderick D. McKenzie (eds.) *The City*. Chicago: University of Chicago Press.

Parker, Karen F., and Patricia L. McCall. 1999. "Structural Conditions and Racial Homicide Patterns: A Look at the Multiple Disadvantages in Urban Areas." *Criminology* 37:447-77.

Parker, Karen F., Patricia L. McCall, and Kenneth C. Land. 1999. "Determining Social-Structural Predictors of Homicide: Units of Analysis and Related Methodological Concerns." Pp. 107-124 in M. Dwayne Smith and Margaret A. Zahn (eds.). *Homicide: A Sourcebook of Social Research*. Thousand Oaks, CA: Sage.

Pedraza, Silvia. 1996a. "American Paradox." Pp. 479-491 in Silvia Pedraza and Ruben G. Rumbaut (eds.). *Origins and Destinies: Immigration, Race, and Ethnicity in America*. Belmont, CA: Wadsworth.

Pedraza, Silvia. 1996b. "Origins and Destinies: Immigration, Race, and Ethnicity in American History." Pp. 1-20 in Silvia Pedraza and Ruben G. Rumbaut (eds.). *Origins and Destinies: Immigration, Race, and Ethnicity in America*. Belmont, CA: Wadsworth.

Portes, Alejandro. 1997. "Immigration Theory for a New Century: Some Problems and Opportunities." *International Migration Review* 31:799-825.

Portes, Alejandro. 2000. "The Hidden Abode: Sociology as Analysis of the Unexpected." *American Sociological Review* 65:1-18.

Portes, Alejandro and Ruban G. Rumbaut. 2001. *Legacies: The Story of the Immigrant Second Generation*. New York: Russell Sage Foundation.

Portes, Alejandro, and Julia Sensenbrenner. 1993. "Embeddedness and Immigration: Notes on the Social Determinants of Economic Action." *American Journal of Sociology* 98:1320-50.

Portes, Alejandro, and Alex Stepick. 1985. "Unwelcome Immigrants: The Labor Market Experiences of 1980 (Mariel) Cuban and Haitian Refugees in South Florida." *American Sociological Review* 493-514.

Portes, Alejandro, and Alex Stepick. 1993. *City on the Edge: The Transformation of Miami*. Berkeley: University of California Press.

Portes, Alejandro, and Cynthia Truelove. 1987. "Making Sense of Diversity: Recent Research on Hispanic Minorities in the United States." *Annual Review of Sociology* 13:359-85.

Romo, Ricardo. 1996. "Mexican Americans: Their Civic and Political Incorporation." Pp. 84-97 in Silvia Pedraza and Ruben G. Rumbaut (eds.). *Origins and Destinies: Immigration, Race, and Ethnicity in America*. Belmont, CA: Wadsworth.

Rose, Harold M., and P. D. McClain. 1990. *Race, Place, and Risk: Black Homicide in Urban America*. Albany: State University of New York Press.

Rosenfeld, Richard, and Scott Decker. 1993. "Discrepant Values, Correlated Measures: Cross-City and Longitudinal Comparisons of Self-Reports and Urine Tests of Cocaine Use Among Arrestees." *Journal of Criminal Justice* 21:223-30.

Rumbaut, Ruben G. 1992. "The Americans: Latina American and Caribbean Peoples in the United States." Pp. 275-307 in Alfred Stepan (ed.). *Americas: New Interpretive Essays*. New York: Oxford University Press.

Rumbaut, Ruben G. 1996. "Origins and Destinies: Immigration, Race, and Ethnicity in Contemporary America." Pp. 21-42 in Silvia Pedraza and Ruben G. Rumbaut (eds.). *Origins and Destinies: Immigration, Race, and Ethnicity in America*. Belmont, CA: Wadsworth.

Rumbaut, Ruben G., Nancy Foner, and Steven J. Gold. 1999. "Immigration and Immigration Research in the United States." *American Behavioral Scientist* 42:1258-63.

Sampson, Robert J. 1987. "Urban Black Violence: The Effect of Male Joblessness and Family Disruption." *American Journal of Sociology* 93:348-82.

Sampson, Robert J., and Janet L. Lauritsen. 1997. "Racial and Ethnic Disparities in Crime and Criminal Justice in the United States," Pp. 311-74 in Michael Tonry (ed.). *Ethnicity, Crime, and Immigration*. Chicago: University of Chicago Press.

Sampson, Robert J., and William Julius Wilson. 1995. "Toward and Theory of Race, Crime, and Urban Inequality." Pp. 37-54 in John Hagan and Ruth D. Peterson (eds.). *Crime and Inequality*. Stanford, CA: Stanford University Press.

Scalia, John. 1996. *Noncitizens in the Federal Criminal Justice System, 1984-1994*. Washington, D.C.: Bureau of Justice Statistics.

Sellin, Thorsten. 1938. *Culture Conflict and Crime*. New York: Social Science Research Council.

Shaw, Clifford R., and Henry D. McKay. 1931. *Social Factors in Juvenile Delinquency*. Washington, DC: U.S. Government Printing Office.

Shaw, Clifford R., and Henry D. McKay. 1969[1942]. *Juvenile Delinquency and Urban Areas: A Study of Rates of Delinquency in Relation to Differential Characteristics of Local Communities in American Cities*. Chicago: University of Chicago Press.

Shihadeh, Edward S., and Nicole Flynn. 1996. "Segregation and Crime: The Effect of Black Social Isolation on the Rates of Black Urban Violence." *Social Forces* 74:1325-52.

Shihadeh, Edward S., and Darrell J. Steffensmeier. 1994. "Economic Inequality, Family Disruption, and Urban Black Violence: Cities as Units of Stratification and Social Control." *Social Forces* 73:729-51.

Short, James F. 1969. "Introduction to the Revised Edition." Pp. xxv-liv in Clifford R. Shaw and Henry D. McKay. *Juvenile Delinquency and Urban Areas: A Study of Rates of Delinquency in Relation to Differential* Characteristics of Local Communities in American Cities. Chicago: University of Chicago Press.

Short, James F. 1997. *Poverty, Ethnicity, and Violent Crime*. Boulder, CO: Westview Press.

Simon, Rita J. 1985. *Public Opinion and the Immigrant:Print Media Coverage, 1880-1980*. Lexington, MA: Lexington Books.

Simon, Rita J. 1993. "Old Minorities, New Immigrants: Aspirations, Hopes, and Fears." *Annals, AAPSS* 530:61-73.

Smith, Dorothy E. 1974. "The Social Construction of Documentary Reality." *Sociological Inquiry* 44:257-67.

Stack, Carol. 1974. *All Our Kin: Strategies for Survival in a Black Community*. New York: Harper and Row.

Stark, Rodney. 1987. "Deviant Places: A Theory of the Ecology of Crime." *Criminology* 25:893-909.

Stepick, Alex. 1998. *Pride Against Prejudice: Haitians in the United States*. Boston: Allyn and Bacon.

Suarez-Orozco, Marcelo M. 1998. "Introduction." Pp. 5-50 in Marcelo M. Suarez Orozco (ed.). *Crossings: Mexican Immigration in Interdisciplinary Perspectives*. Cambridge, MA: Harvard University Press.

Sutherland, Edwin H. 1934. *Principles of Criminology*. Chicago: Lippencott.

Sutherland, Edwin H. 1983[1949]. *White Collar Crime: The Uncut Version*. New Haven: Yale University Press.

Suro, Roberto. 1998. *Strangers Among Us: How Latino Immigration is Transforming America*. New York: Alfred A. Knopf.

Swigert, Victoria Lynn, and Ronald A. Farrell. 1977. "Normal Homicides and the Law." *American Sociological Review* 42:16-32.

Taft, Donald R. 1936. "Nationality and Crime." *American Sociological Review* 1:724-36.

Tanton, John, and Wayne Lutton. 1993. "Immigration and Criminality in the U.S.A." *Journal of Social, Political, and Economic Studies* 18:217-34.

Taylor, Paul S. 1931. "Crime and the Foreign Born: The Problem of the Mexican." Pp. 199-243 in National Commission on Law Observance and Enforcement (ed.). *Report on Crime and the Foreign Born, No. 10*. Washington, D.C.: U.S. Government Printing Office.

Thomas, William I. 1966[1927]. "Situational Analysis: The Behavior Pattern and the Situation." Pp. 154-167 in Morris Janowitz (ed.). *On Social Organization and Personality*. Chicago: University of Chicago Press.

Thomas, William I. 1966[1931]. "The Relation of Research to the Social Process." Pp. 289-305 in Morris Janowitz (ed.). *On Social Organization and Personality*. Chicago: University of Chicago Press.

Thomas, William I., Robert E. Park, and Herbert A. Miller. 1966[1921]. "Assimilation: Old World Traits Transplanted." Pp. 195-214 in Morris Janowitz (ed.). *On Social Organization and Personality*. Chicago: University of Chicago Press.

Thomas, William I., and Florian Znaniecki. 1920. *The Polish Peasant in Europe and America: Volume IV, Disorganization and Reorganization in Poland*. Boston: Gorham Press.

Tonry, Michael. 1995. *Malign Neglect: Race, Crime, and Punishment in America*. New York: Oxford University Press.

Travis, Jeremy. 1997. *A Study of Homicide in Eight U.S. Cities: An NIJ Intramural Research Project*. Washington, DC: National Institute of Justice.

U.S. Commission on Immigration Reform. 1994. *Restoring Credibility*. Washington, D.C.: U.S. Commission on Immigration Reform.

Van Leeuwen, Theo, and Ruth Wodak. 1999. "Legitimizing Immigration Control: A Discourse- Historical Analysis." *Discourse and Society* 1:83-118.

Verniero, Peter, and Paul H. Zoubek. 1999. *Interim Report of the State Police Review Team Regarding Allegations of Racial Profiling*. Copy on file with the author.

Von Hentig, Hans. 1947. Redhead and Outlaw: A Study in Criminal Anthropology." *Journal of Criminal Law and Criminology* 38:1-6.

Waldinger, Roger. 1996. *Still the Promised Land? African-Americans and New Immigrants in Postindustrial New York*. Cambridge, MA: Harvard University Press.

Warner, Barbara D., and Pamela W. Rountree. 1999. "Local Social Ties in a Community and Crime Model: Questioning the Systemic Nature of Informal Social Control." *Social Problems* 44:520-536.

Waters, Mary C. 1999. "Sociology and the Study of Immigration." *American Behavioral Scientist* 42:1264-67.

Waters, Tony. 1999. "Crime and Immigrant Youth." Thousand Oaks, CA: Sage.

Wellman, Barry. 1983. "Network Analysis: Some Basic Principles." *Sociological Theory* 1:155-200.

Weisburd, David, and Tom McEwen (eds.). 1997. *Crime Mapping and Crime Prevention*. Monsey, NY: Criminal Justice Press.

Whyte, William Foote. 1943. "Social Organization in the Slums." *American Sociological Review* 8:34-9.

Wilson, William Julius. 1987. *The Truly Disadvantaged: The Inner City, the Underclass, and Public Policy*. Chicago: University of Chicago Press.

Wilson, Kenneth L., and W. Allen Martin. 1982. "Ethnic Enclaves: A Comparison of the Cuban and Black Economies in Miami." *American Journal of Sociology* 86:295-319.

Winfree, Jr., L. Thomas, and Howard Abadinsky. 1997. *Understanding Crime: Theory and Practice*. Chicago: Nelson-Hall.

Yeager, Matthew G. 1997. "Immigrants and Criminality: A Review." *Criminal Justice Abstracts* 29:143-71.

Yeager, Matthew G. 2002. "Rehabilitating the Criminality of Immigrants Under Section 19 of the Canadian Immigration Act." *International Migration Review* 36:178-192.

Zhang, Pidi, and Jimy Sanders. 1999. "Extended Stratification: Immigrant and Native Differences in Individual and Family Labor." *The Sociological Quarterly* 40:681-704.

Zinsmeister, Karl. 1987. Asians: Prejudice from Top to Bottom." *Public Opinion* 10 (July-August):8-10,59.

Index